Dedicated in love and admiration to
Mari Macauley

Who has triumphed over innumerable internal and
external challenges to her self-esteem and is now
dedicated to helping others do the same

Introduction

In this fast-changing, globally competitive world, our self-esteem has a tough survival course to work through. Nearly everyday, or sometimes several times in one day, our self-esteem can get knocked about. If left unrepaired, some scars can last a lifetime.

Self-esteem is having a good opinion of yourself. It should not be confused with arrogance or vanity. Having high self-esteem is a healthy psychological state – a valuable inner resource that we need to protect.

People with high self-esteem are generally calm, relaxed people who are positive, purposeful, expressive and assertive. They are sociable and cooperative; at home in their well-nourished and well-exercised bodies, and are continually searching for ways and means to improve their behaviour and performance. They do not constantly seek the approval of others and are highly capable of acting independently.

When our self-esteem is low we can become fearful, negative, passive, tense, aggressive, indecisive, self-destructive and unmotivated, and we feel powerless and unworthy. As well as affecting our happiness, low self-esteem also impacts on our work and relationships.

With the odds for success and happiness so heavily weighted against people with shaky self-esteem, you can't afford simply to sit back and patiently hope you will gain personal strength and feelings of self-worth. You need to move into action!

So whether your self-esteem is chronically low or you are just experiencing a trough at the moment, this book provides 365 tips to motivate you to assert your needs and develop your potential for success and happiness.

How to use the *Self-Esteem Bible*

The format of this book is very user-friendly, so you can use it in any way you like. You may want to read one tip a day, read the whole book at once and devise your own plan, or simply dip into it as and when you need it.

Although there is one tip for every day of the year, you will notice that there are no specific time guidelines for completing them. This is because you will be working at your own individual pace. Sometimes you will ignore a tip that is not relevant to you or your lifestyle, and at other times you will want to spend a week or longer working on an exercise. You decide where and when you want to linger. Some tips contain exercises and are therefore a little longer than others, but most are short and will be quick and easy to put straight into practice.

The book is divided into four parts, each covering a different area. Part 1 is concerned with health, as your physical and mental health lays the foundation for the other self-esteem building work that follows. Our self-esteem is always more fragile when we are sick or tired as our defences are down and we don't have our usual capacity to deal with put-downs. So the first step is to get yourself in tip-top condition.

Part 2 deals with personal development; this will equip you with the personal power you need to work on your relationships with others, your career and any other area of your life.

Part 3 looks at how you can form and maintain healthy, positive relationships. This will be helpful if you are being taken for granted, ignored, rejected or unfairly criticized by others, or if your low self-esteem is sabotaging your relationships.

Finally, Part 4 looks at the world of work and provides practical advice to people who are unhappy or unappreciated in their employment, to those looking for a new job, and to those who simply want to improve their work performance by becoming more confident and assertive.

I hope you find this self-esteem-building work as empowering and rewarding as I, and many thousands of others, have done. Good luck!

HEALTH

1 Transform your home into a health farm for a weekend

Fill your fridge with nutritious luxury treats. Include one giant bowl of exotic fresh fruit salad and another of sticks of fresh vegetables. Buy or borrow a variety of exercise, dance, martial arts, Pilates and yoga videos. Plan a programme to watch and work through these. Book yourself onto some new outdoor activity that you have been wanting to try (such as rowing, tennis or sailing) – preferably including a lesson so that you will be challenged mentally as well as physically. Buy some aromatherapy oils to use with an oil burner or to add to your bath. Oils such as camomile, sage, frankincense, neroli and lavender are wonderful for relaxation, while basil, eucalyptus, peppermint, pine and rosemary will help to refresh and energize you. Treat yourself to an extravagant extra such as a seaweed scrub to draw out toxins, or simply give yourself a massage using moisturizing lotion with a few drops of essential oil added. Select some CDs for relaxation sessions and make sure you have lots of large fluffy towels and comfortable clothing washed and ready to wear.

2   Beat the exercise excuses

Perhaps you don't enjoy the gym or that early morning run you never have the time to do. Don't give in – you deserve and need a fit body. Find alternatives. Booking in for a regular class is a good way of committing. Try taking your own music, or a language course or motivational tape, to listen to during your workout at the gym. Alternatively, team up with a friend or colleague you never see enough, and make a weekly date for a walk and talk. Until the habit sticks, reward yourself each time you complete an exercise routine. Your aim is to programme your brain to associate exercise with pleasure instead of pain.

3   Take de-stressing action before you become stressed

Release tension from your body by doing a few quick stretches and gentle head rolls at least every hour. Concentrate on the muscles you know your particular work or lifestyle strains. At the very least, clench your fingers and toes and then gently release them several times.

4   Use meditation to clear your mind at least once a day

Sit or lie in a comfortable supported position. Release tension from your face and head by tightening and releasing your muscles in that region a few times. Close your eyes and focus your whole awareness on your breathing. Visualize your breath as it enters and leaves your body. Continue doing this for a minute or so.

While still following your breathing, centre your attention either on your heart or at a point inside your head in the direct line of the central point between your eyes (where your brain controls your 'fight or flight' response). In time to your breathing, in your mind start saying a mantra. This is a word or short phrase of your choosing. (For example, 'calm', 'at peace' or 'I am being'.) Keep repeating your mantra for as long a time as you can spare. When a thought enters your mind, gently refocus your attention on the meditation point you have chosen and continue saying your mantra in time to your breathing.

5 Cut down your intake of stimulants and depressants

Limit yourself to one caffeine drink a day, cut down on the alcohol and give up cigarettes. Experiment with healthier alternatives until your palate begins to crave them. You'll be surprised at how quickly this can happen. (I would never have believed I could teach myself to enjoy camomile tea – my stomach used to turn at its very smell!)

6 Aim for *quality* sleep, not just the proverbial eight hours

Avoid watching action thrillers and late-night news broadcasts. Instead, feed your mind with peaceful and positive images. Use the last hour of the day to watch or read uplifting and calming programmes or stories. Before going to bed, de-stress your body with a candle-lit warm bath and an all-over self-massage with sandalwood or lavender lotion.

Ensure your bedroom is well aired, as a good supply of oxygen is necessary for body repair work. If you live in a polluted area, treat yourself to an air purifier for your bedroom. Invest in heavy curtains or blackout blinds. The sleep inducing hormone melatonin starts taking effect when darkness descends. Use earplugs or very quiet rhythmic music to block out any distracting noise.

9   Prescribe yourself more fun

Fun encourages healing and builds up resistance to disease. This happens because laughter counters the effects of physical stress and the endorphins that it produces boost the immune system.

10   Buy or pick yourself fresh flowers once a week

Don't wait for someone else to do you this honour or wait for an excuse to give some to your beloved. You deserve to feast on the uplifting and luxurious qualities of natural beauty – all day and every day. Even one or two blooms will do the trick if a bunch is not possible.

12 Timetable 45 minutes of deep relaxation into every week

This is the kind of relaxation that makes you feel as though you're detached from your body and floating in the air. When you are in this deeply tranquil physical state, your body will rebalance itself and carry out any necessary repair work. Experiment with different ways to achieve this state until you find the one that suits you. You could use one of the techniques in this book (for instance, tips 28, 98, and 277) or you may find a particular brand of yoga or meditation works well for you. If this is the case, then stick with this method for as long as you can, because if you do you will find that it takes less and less time to reach the point of deep relaxation.

13   Release pent-up emotions

It may not always be possible to do this at the time your feelings were aroused, but you can do it later. As soon as possible, try to find a private space where you can laugh, cry, scream or thump a cushion. Alternatively, playing a sport or doing certain hobbies can also be a good way to channel unexpressed frustrations.

Take care not to overdo the release. If you find yourself becoming even more angry or sad, stop immediately. Instead, find a friend or a professional counsellor with whom you can talk through the problem. You may need to let go of your feelings gradually, over a long period of time.

14   Have a professional health check

Unless you have had one very recently, make an appointment for a full health check right now. Your doctor, a commercial health insurance company or some fitness trainers can do this.

15 Don't skip your dental check-ups

Bad teeth cause irritation in our digestive systems as well as our mouths. Their infections can also depress our immune system and sap our energy, long before we are aware of any pain. And unkempt teeth do nothing for our self-esteem.

16 Give yourself a fitness lifestyle check once a month

Ask yourself the following questions:

★ What proportion of nights have I had adequate sleep? (Six to eight hours per night for most people.)
★ Have I eaten healthily? (Adequate fresh fruit and vegetables each day and limited fatty, sugary and processed foods.)
★ Have I drunk enough of what is good for me and said 'no' enough to toxic drinks? (Two litres of pure water every day; maximum of two cups of coffee or tea per day and a maximum of three units of alcohol per day.)
★ Have I exercised enough?

17   Watch more comedy

Book tickets to see a funny play, film or comedy show at least once next month. If you can't get out, how about a video or DVD? Comedy takes us out of ourselves and helps us put our little problems in better perspective. And (as if that isn't enough) the laughter it triggers will help strengthen our immune system.

18   Keep up-to-date with health research

Read books and magazines about improving your health. It will help you to prevent many problems as well as getting you to the front of the queue for any new wonder cures.

19   Go green with your own energy

View your energy as a scarce resource to be valued and used economically. Conserve it whenever you can, so you have plenty left for your important projects. (For example, if you have to travel, consider going by train instead of tiring yourself out driving.) Assertively refuse to do things that you don't need or wish to do.

20 Identify your body's stress warning signs

Having a basically bad opinion of yourself makes you even more vulnerable to stress. Get to know and keep a short checklist list of your body's warning signals of stress. Some of us notice our first sign of tension in our back, for others it is in the head or legs. The trick is to know where your area of weakness is, and closely monitor it before the symptom begins to cause serious problems. Write your warning signals out on a card and place them in a prominent position as a constant reminder. Physical symptoms of stress may include:

shoulder, back or neck ache
headaches
indigestion
bowel problems
blocked sinuses
frequent urination
skin rashes
stiffness in joints
frequent pins and needles
dizziness
excessive PMT

21 Know how your behaviour changes under stress

Each of us has developed a habit of behaving in a certain way when we are under stress. You may not be able to see the change in yourself, so you may need someone else to give you feedback. Here are some examples of common habits:

poor concentration
insomnia
nail-biting, scratching and picking
inability to listen attentively
talking too much
inability to control giggling
being reclusive
rushing around
shouting more than usual
clumsiness
difficulty making decisions
poor planning leading to over-tight schedules
reluctance to delegate
unkempt appearance
missing exercise workouts
not spending time on hobbies
empty social diary
being over-protective
playing it too safe
overspending and mounting debt
getting up or going to bed too late
nightmares
forgetting more than usual
missing appointments or birthdays

22   Know your emotional stress warning signs

Just as each of us responds to stress in an individual way with our bodies and behaviour, our emotions also change. Some of us become uptight while others become anxious. These emotional responses are shaped by our genes and early childhood experiences. They are often very inappropriate responses to the kind of stressful situations we meet in adulthood. We need to be aware of these automatic emotional reactions so that we can control them before acting on them. Identify the feelings you experience most commonly when you first become stressed. Here are some examples of emotional response to stress:

irritability
over-excitability
apathy
tearfulness
uncontrollable worrying
anxiety attacks
decrease in confidence
increase in obsessions or phobias
palpitations
feelings of being overwhelmed or confused
a feeling of powerlessness
a feeling of watching the world from the outside
loss of trust in people

23   Cut down rather than cut out during times of pressure

Rather than imposing a punishing total ban on de-energizing foods and drinks, cut them down and strictly limit your intake to certain periods of the day. While you are working, take nutritious snacks rather than big meals.

24   Don't sit still for more than an hour

Your body was not designed to be chair-bound. It will tell you so with backache and headaches. So if you are working at a desk, take regular short breaks in which you physically release your tension by stretching, walking around or, better still, running up and down stairs a couple of times.

25   Respect your own biorhythms

You probably already know whether you are a 'morning' or 'evening' person. But our body's energy levels dip up and down in a fairly regular individual pattern throughout the day. Observe yours and use your cycles to your best advantage. Keep your creative tasks for times when you have most energy, and your household chores or administrative tasks for other times.

For example, I have a low period mid-morning, so that's when I do some easy admin work. To cope with my afternoon low period, I arrange my life so that short siestas are usually possible.

26   Go easy on yourself in times of change

Remember only certain changes can be as good as a rest; most are extremely high on energy consumption and you will need to make a big allowance for this fact.

27   Avoid overdosing on media models of perfection

You can easily set yourself up to feel inadequate, even if your head knows that you are really OK. For example, if you are trying to lose a mere half stone, don't keep buying magazines in which the models are all a few stone lighter than you need to be. Don't gaze too long at photos of glamorous celebrities with unlimited incomes just before you go shopping with a restricted but adequate budget.

28   **Find quick-fix relaxation techniques that work for you**

Try one of my favourites tricks. Lie down with your eyes shielded (or sit in a supported tension-free position with your eyes closed). Take three deep slow breaths and count backwards from 50. As soon as your mind begins to wander, return to 50 until you reach the number one without stopping. Bring a calming image into your mind's eye (for example, a landscape scene, animal or person) and just focus on it for another minute.

30   Build your inner strength

Join a class such as Pilates or Alexander Technique. These concentrate on strengthening the internal muscles that support your back. You will find that you are 'walking tall' without having to think about it.

31 Watch yourself in supermarkets

Supermarkets are notorious for 'helping' us buy what we don't need or even want. Don't risk feeling stupid about having bought too much or finding your trolley full of foods you shouldn't eat. Before entering the store, make a list and stick to it firmly. Order your list to fit in with the store's lay-out (for instance, if vegetables are in the first aisle, place them at the top of the list). This will stop you wandering all over the shop and coming across more temptation. Setting yourself a time limit in the store can also help. If you must, allow yourself a certain amount of money for spontaneous purchases.

32 Give yourself a health warning when you get irritated

Some injustices are undoubtedly worth getting furious over, but the majority of life's minor frustrations are not. This may be true even when we think we have good cause to feel annoyed.

One very sound reason for not staying angry is that it can damage you. If you need a quick way to wind down and encourage yourself to forgive or forget, just remind yourself that the build-up of tension produced by anger can:

★ cause or exacerbate digestive disorders;
★ create hypertension;
★ raise our cholesterol levels;
★ damage and block our arteries;
★ aggravate heart disease;
★ exacerbate bowel disorders such as colitis;
★ increase our susceptibility to infection;
★ intensify pain;
★ create headaches and exacerbate sinus conditions;
★ contribute to inflammatory disorders of the muscles;
★ hinder our recovery from major traumas and illnesses.

33   Be kind to yourself when you have reason to be sad

If you are truly sad, it rarely helps to tell yourself to 'snap out of it'. You can only cover up sadness this way. The danger then is that you may become depressed or your bottled-up feelings may re-emerge at a highly inconvenient time.

Try instead to set aside some private time to heal and feel your blues. Close the door, switch off your phone and have a few hours of intensive nurturing. For example, you might choose to make yourself a meal of comfort foods, put on some quiet, uplifting music, have a soak in the bath and then retire early to bed with a light absorbing novel or video. If tears emerge, cry them out. Don't worry that once you start they will never stop. Crying is a natural by-product of sadness and it makes most people feel a good deal better. Equally, don't be too concerned if you cannot cry. Unlike the comfort and rest, weeping is not an essential emotional healer.

34 Use your imagination to take yourself on a mini-break

Remember, you can 'get away from it all' anytime you choose. You just need to train your mind to help you do so. Practise this technique regularly, and then use it whenever you need a refreshing break.

Lie or sit in a comfortable, well-supported position. Close your eyes and concentrate on the flow of your breath. Imagine that as it enters your body, it is a warm orange colour and that as it leaves your body, it is a pure iridescent white light. Gradually deepen and slow down the pace of your breathing until your body is feeling deeply relaxed and your mind has started to float.

Use your imagination to take you to one of your favourite relaxation spots – this could be a garden, the seaside or somewhere you spent a peaceful holiday. Notice and enjoy all the scents, sounds, colours and textures of this special place, and imagine the serenity and beauty of this place seeping into the pores of your skin. Focus on one particular object or aspect of your scene while continuing to breathe at a gently rhythmic rate until you feel even more deeply relaxed and glowing with positive energy.

35 Supplement your diet at times of pressure

When the going is tough, it is only human to become more slapdash and lazy with regard to food. Until you have better control of your lifestyle, make sure you take vitamin and mineral supplements. If you cannot digest these easily or dislike taking them, ensure that your pockets are filled with nutritious snacks such as nuts and dried fruits.

36   Replace gloomy predictions with motivational statements

When you find you are about to say something like, 'I'm so lazy. I'll never be able to keep going to the gym ...', say instead, 'I can be persistent and I won't stop trying until I find an exercise routine that works for me.' Should you actually say the put-down out loud, simply smile and say, 'That sort of talk won't help me because I know that I can be persistent and I want to be fit.' Sooner or later you will convince yourself (not to mention the rest of the world!).

37 Get in a sweat three times a week

Research has shown that to maintain a good-enough level of fitness, we need to have 3 periods of about 20 minutes aerobic exercise each week. The exercise should be hard enough to bring you out in a slight sweat, but unless you are training for the Olympics it doesn't need to be any harder.

So don't feel guilty about not taking a daily jog. But if you *can* find an activity that makes you sweat and is also fun, you could gain even more vitality and stamina by doing it every day!

38   Don't ignore everyday encounters with hassle

We often collapse in a heap and are forced to rest after a major trauma. On the other hand, the stressful effects of smaller pressures are usually ignored. Try to get into the habit of finding five minutes to release your tension after each routine hassle such as exacting sales encounters, or getting the children off to school or bed.

39 Chemical calmers can't change your life

Tranquillizers change the way you feel about your life – they don't make it better. Only you can do that. So if you must take them, make sure that you are also dealing with the root causes of your anxiety as well as its symptoms.

40 Stick to your bedtime hour

Try to go to bed at the same hour most days of the week. Research indicates that our bodies need a regular clock and that the most restful sleep comes in the first few hours. So, if you need extra hours in the day, take them early in the morning rather than late at night.

41   Watch what you eat at night

Ensure your bedtime snacks are easily digestible. Keep away from complex proteins and spicy curries. Stick to simple soporific carbohydrates. But do keep an eye on the latest research as well – there are some surprises emerging. Did you know, for example, that it has been proved that lettuce induces sleep? But, then again, you might not fancy salad for a comforting midnight feast!

42   **Keep a worry-pad by your bed**

If you cannot sleep because your head is spinning with worries, put the light back on and quickly jot these down. Sounds too simple a solution but it usually works. You may find your concerns look quite different in the light of the morning. If they don't, at least you'll be in better shape to deal with them after a night's sleep.

43 Get to know your genes

Find out your family's disease and death history. This may sound like a dangerously depressing thing to do. But it is also self-caring and sensible. If you know which particular illnesses you are pre-disposed to develop, there is almost always some preventative step you can now take to reduce your chances of becoming ill in that way.

44   Clean up the air around you

You wouldn't expose a child you loved to poisonous air, but you may be doing just that to yourself. Check your immediate environment – both at home and at work. For example, some household cleaning substances are much more dangerous than others and some 'fresh' air coming through open windows is far from enervating. You could treat yourself to an air purifier instead of simply worrying about the pollution.

45 Ensure that your furniture and equipment is taking care of you

You deserve seats and mattresses that support your back; computers that don't strain your eyes; cars that are built with safety in mind and smoke detectors that work. Don't settle for anything less.

46   Test out alternative therapies and trust the ones that work for you

In spite of all the scare stories and cynicism from traditional sources of medical help in the West, complementary therapies are increasing in popularity. This is partly because consumers are becoming more assertive and more willing and able to research and experiment with options. Taking this kind of responsibility for your own health care is very good for your self-esteem and it rarely endangers your body. A good way to find out more about what is available is to read alternative health magazines; or even better, try to sample it for yourself. You can usually do this at mind/body/spirit festivals and fairs. They are advertised in the press, in local libraries and on the internet. If you find something that works, or a practitioner you trust, stick by your right to decide what is good for you. Don't forget to tell your doctor – the best ones are only too pleased to learn from their patients.

47   Keep a list of favourite re-energizing activities

When we are overtired and listless, we think negatively. We are inclined to feel powerless and are likely to blame anyone but ourselves for causing our current state. This is when it helps to have some reminders of what we can do almost immediately to revitalize our bodies and spirits – in spite of the pressures from our external world.

Your list should not include anything that would be difficult to do or to afford. (Otherwise, your negative side will argue you out of action!) Examples of suitable activities could be:

★   A walk or run in the park;
★   A long hot bath;
★   A fast bracing shower;
★   Half-hour of leisurely gardening;
★   A swimming race with a fun friend;
★   A take-away dinner eaten by candle light;
★   A very early night with a great book or a great person!

48   Beware of treats with a health sting in their tail

Some rewards and cheer-up treats can leave us feeling worse about ourselves. This is because we know they are bad for us. Obviously, we can all have such treats once in a while, but if we overuse them they will inevitably do us more harm than good. So think twice before giving yourself the following kinds of 'treats':

★ The big 'waster booze-up' that leaves you nauseous the next day;
★ The cigarette that you know is clogging up your lungs;
★ The double portion of chocolate cake that tanks up cholesterol and calories;
★ The violent film that deprives you of a good night's sleep;
★ The retail therapy that leaves you with just enough cash for a junk-food supper.

PART 2

PERSONAL
DEVELOPMENT

49   Don't stay too serious

It is very easy to become over-intense about yourself and life when you are engaged in personal development. In order to change, we have to become highly self-aware and seriously reflective about the life we have given ourselves. At the beginning, as you honestly confront some of the bad decisions you have made and the apparent inadequacies of your character, you may find your self-esteem decreasing rather than increasing. To counter this, you need fun – lots of it. If you are wondering why, just test it out. Try worrying about being good enough while you are laughing uncontrollably, dancing wildly or singing your heart out!

So don't hold back because you have been invited to do something just because it seems frivolous or superficial. It might be just the kind of 'waste of time' that you need.

50   View your life as a biographer

This is a hard exercise to do, but well worth it. Imagine that a biographer had been commissioned to write your life story. Would they see it as a comedy, an adventure story, an inspirational heroic tale, a soap opera or a puzzling conundrum with no satisfying conclusion?

Now imagine the kind of biography that *ideally* you would like to be written after your death. Give it a title. It should be one that will sum up concisely the essence of how you would like to be remembered. For example, the subtitle of Tanya Stone's biography of Princess Diana sums up the essence of her – *Princess of the People* (Millbrook Press, 1997), as does the subtitle of Vincent Hardy's biography of Martin Luther King – *The Inconvenient Hero* (Orbis, 1996). Remind yourself of your book title whenever you are reflecting on your current life and future plans.

51   Always have at least one treat to look forward to

Ideally, you should always have one mini-treat each day, a slightly bigger one every week and a bumper one each year. People with low self-esteem rarely treat themselves enough. They wait (and wait!) until they think they really deserve one. Treats are not the same as rewards – you can have plenty of those too. Treats should be considered as simply routine. They are as essential for your mental health as brushing your teeth is for your dental health. So get planning more for yourself.

This will give you a great psychological lift. You will actually see some positive change without having risked too much. You will feel less guilty about having more than you need. And the physical work will energize you and give you a much-needed break from your introspection.

Writing down some rules for yourself before you start will help you to stick to them. For instance, you might:

★ Pass on anything not worn in the past two years;
★ Pass on books never likely to be read;
★ Send every utensil that hasn't been used for the past year to the charity shop;
★ Dispose ecologically of all machines and equipment that you rarely use;
★ Take old magazines to the doctor's surgery.

53 Take up a new hobby

You may not be able to change your job or move house, but there can be no excuse for not starting a new hobby. It should be one you think you could be good at, but that will still be a challenge. Watch out for being over-ambitious. (When our self-esteem is low, we often unconsciously set ourselves up for failure by aiming too high.) Take care that it is one that *you* really want to do – being dragged along to someone else's evening class won't help. If others are likely to view your chosen activity as childish, extravagant or a waste of time, give yourself the permission to do it secretly.

54   Set goal after goal

Every habitual achiever knows how important it is to set goals. Of course, it is possible to have a lifetime of 'lucky breaks', but how probable is it? The chances of having regular success without setting targets for yourself are minimal. Setting goals gives us an inspiring sense of purpose and it fuels our momentum.

Success (albeit on our terms and in our own eyes) is essential for self-esteem. So once you have achieved your target, don't lose any time in setting another goal. It doesn't matter how small or how personal that goal is, as long as it excites you.

55   If you are unhappy, give something up

'When life is not working for you, you are being asked to give up. You are being asked to give up thoughts, beliefs, perceptions, habits and fears that hold you back. There can be no new miracles while you are holding on to the old stuff. Pain is a signal to let go, give something up, open up and try something new.'

ROBERT HOLDEN

56   Timetable self-reflection into your schedule

Serious self-esteem problems don't accrue overnight. They grow gradually – so gradually, in fact, that it is all too easy for us not to notice what is happening. Most people only find out when they meet a setback and find themselves unable to bounce back. Others may not realize how low their self-esteem has got until they become physically ill through being over-anxious about their performance or appearance.

This is why, if you have a tendency to doubt or disrespect yourself, it is important to make self-reflection a routine exercise. The easiest way to do this is to ensure that it is timetabled into your diary. At first, try to make this a daily appointment: 5–10 minutes is all you need. Just ask yourself a few searching questions such as:

★ How do I feel about myself today?
★ What have I achieved?
★ What have I enjoyed?
★ How have I looked after myself?
★ Have I done anything that I regret?
★ Have I been true to my values?
★ Have I been myself?

57   Use strangers' eyes to watch yourself

Although for self-esteem, self-respect is more important than the respect of others, the reality is that most people cannot achieve the first without the second. This is not surprising since essentially we are social animals. Very few of us have either the ability or inclination to live as hermits.

From time to time, take a moment to imagine what people who don't know the 'real you' might think of you. Ask yourself, in the light of your behaviour and appearance, whether they would be likely to respect or disrespect you? You could do this exercise while sitting on a train, standing at an airport queue or after making a purchase in a shop.

Remember, you don't have to share your conclusions with anyone, so be strictly honest with yourself, keeping yourself at the centre of your attention. This is not an exercise in trying to understand or judge anybody. Its purpose is simply to raise your self-awareness and gently challenge your self-perception.

When inhaling the scent of a stunning rose, it is hard to feel bad about anything, including yourself. But perhaps other scents have an even more powerfully positive effect on you. Each person is unique in the way that his or her senses respond to the world.

Now think of your most pleasurable sights, smells, tastes, sounds and textures. Vow to give yourself more exposure to each and to experiment with new sensual experiences. The more options you have, the less excuse there will be to deny yourself these important pleasures.

59   By being kind to yourself, you also open doors

'Learning how to be kind to ourselves, learning how to respect ourselves, is important. The reason that it is important is that when we look into our own hearts, it isn't just ourselves we are discovering.

'We are also discovering the universe.'

ANE PEMA CHÖDRÖN

60   Rediscover the joy and satisfaction of creativity

Creativity plays a vital role in boosting our self-esteem. Think about how pleased with yourself you are when you make something new or come up with an innovative idea or design. If you don't think of yourself as a particularly creative person, reflect for a moment on your childhood. You would have to have been a *very* strange child if you didn't enjoy making something? Did you like building, drawing or staging plays? If so, maybe there is still part of you that could be developed through taking up a new hobby such as DIY, painting or amateur operatics.

But don't limit yourself to artistic pursuits. Of course, artists do tend to be highly creative in their work, but then so are many scientists, technicians, labourers and service providers in theirs. Also, many people think creativity has to produce a new 'thing'. In fact, creativity can also be used to produce a more innovative, interesting, or enjoyable process or for-mat. For instance, one office manager may make the pro-duction of an annual report into a predictable routine chore, while another might find an innovative way each year to collect and present more or less the same material.

Finally, don't forget that you can use your creativity to help you save money. You could, for example, make your own Christmas cards and presents, or re-model old clothes, furniture or cars. And then you could set about 're-vamping' yourself with the money you save!

61 Visualize your life dream

Allow yourself ample relaxed uninterrupted time to day-dream and gaze into your personal crystal ball. Try to conjure up a vivid picture in your mind's eye of the kind of life you would like to see yourself leading in, say, 5, 10 or 20 years' time. Watch yourself enjoying your dream in full Technicolor as though you were watching a movie. At the same time, try to hear any sounds and smell the scents that accompany your imagined image. Doing this will fix the picture of your dream in your subconscious. Once it is there your brain will automatically help you find opportunities to make your dream come true. When it 'sees' the outside world, it immediately highlights stimuli that match the information already programmed into your mind. This is why we literally 'see what we want to see and hear what we want to hear'. Should your life dream feature, for example, snow-capped mountains, don't be surprised to find that your eye automatically is drawn to the one and only book in the shop that happens to be called *Teach yourself Mountaineering!*

62   Talk about your dream

You can also ensure that your friends and acquaintances help you to make your dream come true. The more you talk about your hopes and future plans, the more they are likely to notice helpful opportunities and introduce you to the kind of people you need to meet. I remember unexpectedly finding a friend's dream house for her. Because she had vividly described her ideal home, when a picture of a certain farmhouse appeared in the paper it caught my eye. I wasn't consciously searching for houses for her, but obviously my unconscious was very busy being helpful!

63 Steer clear of the 'deep end' of challenges

A common habit of people with low self-esteem is to highlight the hardest and most complex part of any problem first. So watch yourself! For example, should you be feeling isolated and sidelined in a new office, stop yourself from trying to attract the attention of the busiest person around. Or, should you be given a book list for a new course, don't start by reading the heaviest academic tome first. Always start at 'the shallow end' when trying to overcome a difficulty or attempt to learn something new. Overcome the mini-challenges first, then you will have the motivation and self-confidence to deal with the worst.

64   Don't wait until you are feeling ugly to enhance your beauty

If you go along to the hairdresser when your hair is in a desperately unkempt state, you will not have the confidence to insist on the cut that you really want and know suits you best. If you wait until your complexion is spotty and sallow before booking yourself a facial or weekend of sunshine, how can you expect to enjoy the experience?

Make a personal policy to give yourself regular treats that leave you feeling and looking more beautiful or handsome.

65 Keep stretching the strengths of your intellect

Most of us only use a tiny fraction of our brain's potential. Research has confirmed that we can develop our intellect at any age. It may take us a little longer to learn as we get older, but we can still learn virtually anything at any age. But it is a lot easier and more satisfying to keep your learning in tune with your intellectual strengths. So, for example, if you are good at problem solving do more crosswords, or if you have a good memory you could start learning a new language. Unless you *need* to stretch an area of weakness, leave it alone. (Years ago, I made a decision to stop feeling guilty about using calculators to do any and every calculation. I am sure I will live a good deal longer as a result!)

66 **Turn the clock forward to check you are on track**

If you want to be the kind of person who can look back at the end of their life with pride and satisfaction, try doing this exercise from time to time. Imagine you are 80-years old and someone is giving a speech about you and your wonderful personal qualities. Which six qualities would you be most proud to hear them praise you for?

Beside each of your six qualities, write what you need to do in order to live more in harmony with each right now. For example:

Honesty   I need to be more honest about the fact that I am not enjoying being with Jean as much as I once did.

Caring   I need to spend more time with Dad.

67   Know what lifts your spirits – and do more of it!

Keep a note of the activities that you find lift your spirits and make you feel good about simply being alive. For example, this could be playing with your own or someone else's children, spending a day by the sea, playing a game of tennis or golf, or simply lounging on the sofa watching a DVD. Look at your list every so often and check that you are doing some of these. Keeping adding to the list when you have an experience that you notice has refreshed your spirit.

68   **Keep humour handy**

Place some books of comic poetry and verse or funny short anecdotes by your bed and in the bathroom. Dip into them before going to sleep, on waking and when relaxing in the bath. These are important times for influencing your subconscious and this will help set you in a positive fun mode for the next day.

Collect tips from inspirational people who have battled against the odds to achieve. Keep a pad by the radio and TV and aim to write down at least one a week. There is no shortage of interviews with courageous people. You can choose to be overawed by their outstanding achievements or you can be encouraged and uplifted by their achievements. Here are some examples I have collected this way myself:

> *'To be a father of a nation is a great honour, but to be a father of a family is a greater joy. But it was a joy I had far too little of.'*

> NELSON MANDELA – ON HIS SUCCESSES AND REGRETS

> *'Fear of failure is a great energiser – if you can master it, you can do anything in any profession.'*

> ROD STEIGER – ON THE UPS AND DOWNS OF HIS LIFE

> *'I've always just been me. What you see is what you get.'*

> SALLY GUNNELL – OLYMPIC CHAMPION

> *'I've learned to trust life and that if you persist, it will get better. I also think it is also important to believe in something.'*

> ROSIE BOYCOTT – JOURNALIST, ON HER RECOVERY
> FROM DRUG AND ALCOHOL ADDICTION

70　Secretly record compliments that move you

Most people with low self-esteem are terrified of becoming big-headed, so this will be a difficult exercise. But I am (for the moment!) granting your fear one concession – you can do your compliment recording in secret.

Do try this tip, because by writing it down and re-reading it later, the compliment will have a much better chance of boosting your self-esteem. Often our embarrassment wipes any compliment clean from our mind the moment it is uttered. Knowing you have this task to do, should help you to remember.

71   Try, try and try again

You have heard this countless times before but you still may not have heard it enough. Low self-esteem erodes our persistence. We often feel like giving up before we have even begun. This is especially true if we know that someone else has tried and failed. So make it a rule never to turn down any opportunity to do something new, just because the idea has been tried out before. With your newly increased self-esteem it has an even better chance of working the second (or tenth!) time around.

'We cannot live only for ourselves. A thousand fibres connect us with our fellow men; and among those fibres, as sympathetic threads, our actions run as causes, and they come back to us as effects.'

HERMAN MELVILLE

73 Don't over-commit your caring side

People with low self-esteem usually do too much caring for others and not enough for themselves. So watch this tendency in yourself. Firstly, if you over-commit, you could wear out not just your body but your spirit too. Even the kindest people can become resentful when they are worn out or begin to have their willingness to commit taken for granted.

Secondly, remember that when we over-commit ourselves, we tend not to function very efficiently. Consequently, your self-esteem will suffer as you notice that you are not keeping up to your usual standards.

People with high self-esteem see treats as essential and give these to themselves frequently. Interestingly, they do not make a big deal about doing so. Treats are ordinary everyday experiences for them. They do not think it is odd, for example, to take some time out on their own to enjoy a book, however busy they are, or to buy themselves mini-presents, however strained their budget is.

Until this habit becomes well-entrenched, keep a check on yourself by inserting a small symbolic mark in your diary or calendar each time you give yourself a treat. You can then review your progress each month.

75   Talk encouragingly to yourself

Follow the lead of successful athletes and sports stars and use encouraging self-talk. Tell yourself when you are doing well or have made a good effort. Remind yourself of the rewards that lie ahead if you persist in trying. Doing this will definitely enhance both your motivation and your performance – and don't forget that talking negatively to yourself will do the opposite. Whenever possible, speak out loud using a positive and energized tone.

Start very safely and do not ever risk life or limb. For example, you could start by changing the way you are interacting
with people in everyday situations:

★ Speak to someone at work you would like to meet but
   who hasn't been formally introduced to you.
★ Give a compliment to someone, even if you think they
   might think you are silly or cheeky for doing so.
★ Ring an over-demanding relative and tell them that
   you have changed your mind about going to an event
   or meal with them.
★ Speak your mind at a meeting, knowing that many
   people will disagree with you.

77 Formally forgive yourself for bad decisions

Don't let your self-esteem be eroded by guilt and regret. When you realize you made a bad choice, say something to yourself such as 'I forgive you … You made that decision in good faith at that time. Let's wipe the slate clean and move on.' Then every time it comes back in your mind, just repeat a simple phrase such as 'The slate has been cleaned.' Or 'You're forgiven.' If someone else brings it up, just tell them that you have forgiven yourself and are moving on.

78   **Convert today's regrets into tomorrow's goals**

As soon as you hear yourself starting a sentence such as, 'I wish I had …' or 'If only I could have …', stop right there in your tracks. Rephrase what you were going to say with a sentence beginning:

'Tomorrow, if I have the opportunity to … I will …'

Stay face-to-face with your values

List the six most important values or principles that you would like to be guiding your life. (For example, integrity, independence, compassion, adventure, fun and intimacy.) Write these on a small card and carry the card around with you for the next few weeks. Read the list often – this will ensure that they are in the forefront of your mind. You cannot have good self-esteem if you disrespect your own values.

80   Visualize *all* options before making a choice

Even when a choice seems simple to you, imagine the outcome of each option before making your decision. Visualize the various possible outcomes in your mind. Take time to see yourself in your mind's eye in each situation. You may surprise yourself. People with low self-esteem tend to play too safe and choose options that are familiar. So next time you hear yourself saying 'I couldn't possibly do that or wear that', run some mental movies in your head before making your final choice.

81 Start a savings plan for 'rainy day' treats

We can never know when life is going to take a nasty turn. Make sure that you are financially able to cheer yourself up. Being able to dip into a ready-made nest egg for a little luxury before you face the problem, could make all the difference. A dose of quality self-love is just what you need to inspire you to cope with a difficult challenge.

82   Read inspirational life stories

Visit your local library one afternoon and browse in the autobiography or biography sections. Dip in and out of books about inspiring people from a wide variety of backgrounds. Note down the ones that move or fascinate you most. Then borrow some to read over the next few weeks.

83 Buy yourself a small book of motivational quotes

Slip it into your pocket or handbag. Whenever you have an odd moment to spare (in one of those boring queues, for instance), read one or two to pep you up. Better still, try to memorize the best, then you will find it pops up into your mind just when you need an extra dose of support and inspiration.

People with high self-esteem thrive on change because they trust that they can make the best of a new situation. But remember, this is another chicken and egg situation – the more opportunities you have to cope well with change the more your self-esteem grows.

Don't hang about waiting for a change to happen so that you can use it to build your confidence. Instead, each day try to make a small alteration to your normal routine. For example, leave home 10 minutes earlier than usual to take a more scenic route; have a better quality lunch in a more lively location; take half an hour to sit down with a great book and refreshing drink before cooking dinner; or drop in to see a friend on the way home from work. This will help you keep more psychologically flexible and ensure you will not feel threatened when a big change arrives.

85   Set yourself conversation homework

If your self-esteem is low, it is likely that you have been avoiding social conversation like the plague. Don't let yourself get away with this. If you stop talking to people, you'll lose whatever social skills you have already developed. It is all too easy to become socially phobic. Force yourself to keep in practice. Make it a rule that you must initiate a conversation with three people every week and try to ensure you talk for a minimum amount of time (say, 5–10 minutes). Don't worry too much about the subject of your conversation. It doesn't have to be a first-class debate – it merely has to keep going. Remember, if the other person doesn't want to converse they can always stop talking themselves.

86   **Write out your life dreams in the present tense**

This is another technique for fixing an inspiring positive future image of yourself in your brain. Try one of these exercises – or even both!

a) Write a not-to-be-mailed letter to a friend or relative describing your dream life using the present tense.
b) Write an imaginary excerpt from a future diary.

Read what you have written aloud several times in the next week. This will further reinforce the image in your mind.

87 Battle with your bad habits, one at a time

Make a list of the bad habits you want to break because they are damaging your self-esteem. Then re-arrange your list in hierarchical order according to the degree of challenge they present. Highlight the one that is the least challenging to tackle first.

Make a resolution not even to attempt to deal with any others until you have broken this one. Make your choice clear to those around you. If anyone should 'have a go at you' for any other bad habit, simply thank them for their concern and say that it is on your list to be dealt with later.

88   Use your personal strengths to overcome bad habits

It is easy to forget our personal strengths when we are over-ly conscious that we are doing something that we would prefer not to be doing. But once you have brought your strengths to mind, think how each could help you in your battle with the habit. For example:

★ Sense of humour – give me some light relief when the going gets too serious and tough.
★ Creativity – come up with new ideas.
★ Good listener – gather wisdom from others who have overcome this habit.

89 Formulate strategies to break bad habits

The more business-like you are in the way that you approach your habit-breaking, the more success you will have. In fact, it is almost pointless to make a resolution without an action plan. Set yourself some dated targets so that you can progress at a realistic rate and in an efficient strategic manner.

90   Commit your plans to paper

Just seeing your plans in black and white increases your chances of success. (Humans do tend to believe what they see with their own eyes!) The act of writing it all down also makes it feel like a more serious commitment and helps to fix it more firmly in the memory bank in our brain.

91 Share your good intentions with a supportive friend

The key here is to choose your friend carefully – it must be someone who really wants you to break this habit. Some 'friends' actually have an investment in other people keeping their bad habits because it makes them feel better about themselves or their bad habits. (You can see the satisfied smile on the face of some people when you hear them say things like: 'I knew you'd never be able to do it' or 'We all have to have a little weakness – yours is smoking, mine is eating chocolate.')

92   Carry a symbolic reminder

It is hard breaking habits so we need all the help we can get. Don't think of yourself as weak-minded if you need a little extra help. A useful trick for keeping you on course is to have a kind of mascot to boost your confidence in your ability to succeed.

Choose something small that you can discreetly carry around with you for the first few crucial weeks. This could be a photo of an inspirational person or an object that will remind you of your goal. For example, if you were trying to cut down on your consumption of beer, you could carry a small picture of a sports star who you know keeps good control of his drinking habits. If you were trying to stop biting your nails, you could carry around a mini-bottle of nail polish to remind you of the manicure you are going to give yourself as a reward.

93 Celebrate overcoming a bad habit in style

Once we have conquered a bad habit it is tempting to try and put it behind us and not to think about it again. But, for the sake of your self-esteem, make sure that you have a celebration even if overcoming the habit may not seem that significant in the light of other problems in your life. You must celebrate victories over *anything* that has been harming your self-esteem.

94   Make public announcements when you kill a bad habit

The fear of the shame you could bring on yourself if you slip back into your old ways will act as a deterrent. Also, if you have told the right kind of people, they will encourage you later by saying things like 'I see you are still not smoking – well done.' or 'I have been looking at your nails with envy – they look fantastic.'

95   Be on guard for your habit's early warning signals

Never become complacent about bad habits – they can creep back so easily. The times when they will be most likely to do so are when you are under stress or when your self-esteem has just been knocked. (Just when you didn't need any more trouble!) Because you may be preoccupied with other things, you may not even notice you are being tempted back into your old ways. It will be a good deal easier to deal with, however, if you have identified a few key early warning signals (such as noticing cigarette advertisements or not bothering to manicure your nails). It might also help you to inform your friends so they can be on guard as well.

96   Use affirmations

Affirmations are short positive statements that we say to ourselves on a regular basis. They can be used to bolster us up when we know we are going into difficult situations or are about to spend time with people who are likely to make us feel small or depressed. Speak them out aloud whenever possible, using a strong, assertive tone. Relax and smile while you are speaking. Here are some examples:

★ I am a positive person;
★ I enjoy challenges;
★ I am a good organizer;
★ I am creative in my approach to problem solving;
★ I take care to maintain my relationships;
★ I am learning from this experience;
★ I decide what can hurt my feelings and what will not.

98 'Anchor' your good feelings in your body

Anchoring is a very powerful technique for storing good feelings in your body so that they can be recalled quickly when we need them. Follow these instructions carefully.

First, you must put yourself into a deeply relaxed state. Then recall, in as much detail as possible, an experience from the past that boosted your self-esteem. Use your imagination to relive the experience slowly and fully, physically and emotionally. Try to recapture the memory of the sensations you felt in your body, including the scents you could smell and the sounds you could hear. Spend a few minutes enjoying this experience while at the same time making a small movement, such as lightly squeezing or tapping a part of your body. (This 'trigger movement' should be discreet so that you will be able to do it in public without anyone noticing.) Repeat this procedure every day for a few weeks. You should then find that you automatically re-awaken your positive high self-esteem feeling as soon as you use your physical trigger.

Experiment as soon as possible with using this anchor in difficult real-life situations. The more often you use the anchor, the more powerful and useful it will be.

Think of yourself as a product for sale

Imagine that in one or two years' time you are going to put yourself up for sale and that you have been asked to submit a brief description of yourself to be included in a glossy brochure. This will be (of course!) an improved version of the current you.

Write a brief introductory paragraph of you and your achievements, and also a brief description of how you would look in the imaginary photograph.

Keep this somewhere where you can look at it from time to time.

100　Exercise one of your strengths each day

List your six main character strengths and allocate each a day for an exercise. (You are allowed a day of rest!) For example, caring – you could ring your parents to see how they are and offer your help to your elderly neighbour; organized – you could plan a party or sort out your cupboards. By the seventh day, you should be feeling very much better about yourself.

101 Talk about times when you felt good about yourself

Does your partner or closest friend know *every*thing you have done that you are proud of? It is highly unlikely. Review your life year by year, recalling times when you did well and felt good about being you. List these examples and share them. You could make it a joint exercise. No one has so much self-esteem that they cannot benefit from sharing in this way.

102   **Start having an 'Affirmation of the week'**

Each Saturday or Sunday morning, decide which aspect of yourself you would like to improve over the following week. It could be a characteristic that will be particularly useful at present. For example, if you are fearing being made redundant or having a change of role imposed upon you, you might choose an affirmation such as 'I am adaptable' or 'I enjoy new experiences'.

Write your affirmation on a postcard and keep it in your bag or diary, or make it into a screen saver on your computer. Read it whenever you begin to worry. By the end of the week you will have convinced yourself.

103 Don't deny your weaknesses to yourself

Even if you have a tendency to put yourself down, you may need some help in spotting this kind of behaviour. If you have a weakness that you feel is very much out of control or one that you are ashamed about, you may well defend yourself unconsciously with 'denial behaviour'. An example of this might be continually repairing zips on jeans that in reality are too small (or you are too big!), rather than just buying a new pair in a larger size. Another might be convincing yourself that you are too tired to go a party when the reality is that you are too nervous.

Discuss this idea of denial with a friend and see if together you can identify some behaviours and excuses that you could watch out for. At the same time, make a resolution to take some positive action to help you with your weakness.

104 Pause the moment a guilt button is pushed

If a criticism immediately makes you gulp with guilt, stop before taking any action. Think of the pain of guilt as being positive – it is there to help you. It is indicating that you might not be living in line with your own values (and you know that self-esteem suffers unless we do this). Pausing will give you a chance to take a slow deep breath and THINK before speaking. It rarely helps to knee-jerk into action in response to guilt. If we do we can be overly apologetic or defensive. Instead, thank the critic for the feedback and acknowledge that you have that weakness. In certain circumstances, (such as with your partner or a colleague,) it may also be wise to add what you are doing to correct that weakness or recompense for any damage done.

105 Don't unnecessarily highlight your weaknesses to others

As you probably know, people with low self-esteem often bring trouble upon themselves. Perhaps you are so aware of your weaknesses that you think they are staring everyone else in the face. The reality is that the vast majority of other people are too preoccupied with other things to notice your spots, paunch, clumsiness, bald patch or skinny legs. So watch out for unnecessary self-disclosures such as, 'You can't miss me. I'm the fat one with the raucous laugh.' or 'I only got here just on time again. I'm so lazy – I just can't get up in the mornings.'

106   Don't compare yourself unfavourably to others

This is usually an entrenched bad habit of people with low self-esteem. You may not even think of it as a bad habit. You are probably just aware of being envious and nice to others because you think you are giving them a compliment. Here are some examples:

★ 'I wish I could cook as well as you do.'
★ 'My presentations are never as creative as that.'
★ 'You always look so immaculate – I just wish that I wasn't so scruffy.'
★ 'That was an incredible shot. Never in a million years, could I match that.'

If you want to give a compliment, give a straight one without including any comparison to you. Not only will your self-esteem miss a knock, the other person will be free to enjoy their compliment. They won't feel manipulated into feeling sorry for you and rescuing you with a patronizing compliment ('Well, you do make a very good cup of tea.').

This exercise will help you to accept your imperfections and the restraints on your personal power. List your weaknesses and taking three different coloured pens, mark the ones that:

a) you cannot change;
b) you could change but they are not worth expending the energy because you can live with them;
c) the weaknesses you want to change.

When you are next confronted with a weakness, check what colour coding it has before taking any action or allowing yourself to feel bad.

108 Look for the positive aspects in your weaknesses

You may not be able to do this for all weaknesses, but it should work for the vast majority. It may help to discuss this exercise with a positive friend who values you and knows you very well.

For each weakness, write a sentence that assertively acknow-ledges it, but also highlights a compensatory feature. For example:

★ 'I accept that I am not a great conversationalist, but because I don't talk much, I am a good listener and often pick up what others miss.'
★ 'I accept that I am bossy, but I can be relied upon to get people moving fast in an emergency situation.'

109 Make a resolution if you start wishing you were different

The most effective way of controlling negative thoughts about yourself is to replace them with a positive statement. The technique will be doubly effective if you make a resolution at the same time. For example:

✗ 'I wish I was as fit as I was a few years ago.'

replace with

✓ 'I will walk up the stairs at work every day.'

✗ 'I wish I was more courageous.'

replace with

✓ 'I will take a small risk every day and note it down in my diary.'

110 Stop exaggerations of your faults with reality checks

You may not be able to stop unnecessary exaggerations coming out of your mouth, but you can replace them immediately with a more accurate statement. At first, you may need someone to help you spot them but soon you will hear them yourself. Here are some examples:

After forgetting to post a letter:

✗   'I am the most forgetful person on earth – I can't remember anything these days.'

replace with

✓   'Actually this is the first time this week that I have forgotten to take the post with me.'

On being overweight:

✗   'Look at me I'm gross.'

replace with

✓   'I am 2 kg heavier than I want to be, but I will exercise these off this year.'

112 Acknowledge the positive in every mistake

You may think it is impossible to find a positive element in every mistake, but try it out before you dismiss this tip. If the answer is 'yes' to any of these questions, you've cracked it:

★ 'Did I learn anything from this experience?'
★ 'Could making this mistake prevent me from making a bigger one later?'
★ 'Do I now know more about my potential or limitations?'
★ 'Could any other deserving person benefit from my mistake?'

113 Acknowledge the things you do better than other people

This is a hard one to do when your self-esteem is low, but it is very good medicine. Don't worry about becoming too big-headed. That is highly unlikely to be one of your problems – ever!

Remember that it doesn't matter how insignificant or useful your skill may seem to be in the big wide world. You are not trying for a Nobel prize, you are simply doing essential repair work on your self-esteem. If you can do this exercise with a group of friends or colleagues, it can be very revealing. You'll be surprised how many hidden talents people have. Examples of undervalued talents I have heard being shared are:

★ spotting butterflies;
★ growing peas;
★ solving crossword puzzles;
★ making up children's stories;
★ finding bargain holidays.

You could even start counting them each day. You will probably be surprised by how many you will be able to list.
People with low self-esteem often rate themselves high
on selfishness. This is because they know they are overly
self-absorbed. When you feel better about yourself you will
have more energy to give out to others, but for the moment
at least, acknowledge the good that you are able to do right
now.

Deal with the fear and do it anyway

Almost anything worth doing has an element of risk attached to it. Listen to successful people being interviewed – they almost always reveal that they were frightened by the challenges they took up. One of the big differences between them and less successful people is their determination to deal constructively with their fear. They may take control of it by doing some form of relaxation (such as a diversion activity or exercise) or by re-directing their mind to positive thoughts. You could learn to do what they do by using one of the many techniques such as Affirmations and Visualizations, contained in this book (see tips 96, 102 and, 308). Then, for even more ideas on mastering fear, you could read Susan Jeffers' excellent book *Feel the Fear and Do It Anyway* (… and apologies to Susan for re-writing her famous title at the top of this page!)

116 Take more initiative

You probably stifle most of your good ideas in favour of giving others a voice first. No doubt you have also often kicked yourself later when you hear your undeclared proposal coming out of another's mouth.

Next time you hear a message in your head saying something like 'They think I'm stupid for suggesting this', 'Who is going to listen to me I'm only …' or 'Supposing, it doesn't work', replace it with a permission statement such as ' I have a right to be heard even if I am wrong' or 'My ideas do deserve a chance'.

117 Like celebrities, transform your appearance regularly

You also want to be noticed and admired. (Hard to admit maybe, but isn't it true?) So take a leaf from the celebrity book and change the way you look reasonably frequently. This doesn't mean that you too have to indulge in expensive professional makeovers or become a fashion victim. However, you could think about altering your hair, changing the dominant colour you wear or buying a new hat or striking tie.

119 Imagine that you have only three weeks to live

Think how you would spend that time. Ask yourself:

★ Who would you like to share it with?
★ Where would you like to visit?
★ What would you like to say that you haven't said?
★ What would you like to finish?

Now, bearing your answers in mind, make a list of your priorities for the next month.

120   Check you give your needs appropriate attention

The psychologist Abraham Maslow's famous 'Hierarchy of Needs' triangle (see below) could help you to give your needs appropriate attention. He suggested that our human needs tend to develop on a scale from one to five. At the bottom are our basic survival needs and at the top our 'luxury' needs. In order to feel good about ourselves and function at our best, we need to ensure that we are dealing with our needs in the right order – from the bottom to the top. You could be making life very hard for yourself if you are trying to meet your 'top' needs while the bottom ones remain unfulfilled. Test it out by skipping a couple of meals and then trying to concentrate on a book or rich piece of music!

Self-fulfilment
Self-expression
Belonging
Security: shelter and warmth
Physiological needs: hunger, thirst and health

121 Start each day by feeding your mind with positive food

Your subconscious mind is very impressionable in its waking moments. The thoughts and experiences you give it in the first hour can establish your basic mood for the day. If you start your day worrying, arguing, listening to depressing news or moaning about the weather, you are setting yourself up for a less enjoyable day than perhaps you need or deserve. So start the day doing something you enjoy such as listening to music, having a soak in the bath, playing with the children or reading a chapter of a good book.

If your family or life circumstances are currently stressful, set your alarm 20 minutes earlier and use that time quietly on your own, again doing something you enjoy.

122 Keep yourself well informed about current facts and trends

This means that you will be ready to join in many more social conversations. Have a notepad handy by the radio or TV to jot down interesting facts and unusual statistics. Re-read them every couple of days. Doing this will ensure that you remember them better. Your self-esteem will shoot up at least one notch when you see other people's faces light up with interest.

123 Value your simple successes

To laugh often and much;
to win the respect of intelligent
people and the affection of children;
to earn appreciation of honest critics and endure
the betrayal of false friends;
to appreciate beauty;
to find the best in others;
to leave the world a bit better,
whether by a healthy child,
a garden patch or a
redeemed social condition;
to know even one life has
breathed easier
because you have lived.
This is to have succeeded.

RALPH WALDO EMERSON

It is so easy to say to yourself 'There's always tomorrow' as an excuse for not doing what you would like to do or need to do today. Face yourself with the reality that the 'tomorrow' you anticipate may never come. You may not have the opportunity to do what you put off today ever again.

125 Listen to your intuition, but check it out too

Remember 'gut feelings' are not necessarily good intuition. Intuition is wisdom that is stored deep in the brain and accessed by our right brain without us having to analyze (with our left hemisphere) the facts and figures of a situation. Our right brain has the capacity to scan and collate (subconsciously) a wide range of different kinds of information, memories and feelings and occasionally come up with a strong match between them. That's when we get a powerful sense of 'deep knowing'. It feels strange because we haven't had to do any conscious thinking work. When it is working well, it can come up with brilliant new ideas and wise guidance that we may never have 'worked out' with our conscious minds.

However, it is important to be aware that if your past has been full of trauma and fear, there will be a good deal of negative data stored in your brain. This will colour the responses of your 'intuition'. Consequently, you may feel too many unwarranted gut warnings about people and opportunities. That is why you need to be particularly careful to check out your intuitive response before taking or not taking action.

One quick way of doing this is to ask yourself if this current situation 'feels' familiar. If it does, think back to the persons or events that also gave you a similar feeling and use your left-brain analytical powers to compare the past with the current situation. If they are very different, you may want to ignore your gut and seize today's opportunity.

You can do this by reading books or watching films that provide practice in finding connections between different phenomena (for example, thrillers and murder mysteries or biographies that attempt to understand their subjects from a psychological, biological and sociological point of view). You could also enrol in a class that will help you do this (perhaps one that takes a look at art, TV, films or events in their historical, cultural, political and religious contexts).

127 Analyse your hunches

Think of an occasion when you followed a hunch with great success (perhaps a time when you selected a new friend from a crowd of strangers; an unexplored holiday destination or an idea for a new business venture). Then think of a hunch that you followed that didn't turn out to be so insightful. Compare the two occasions using your analytical side to note what kind of information your right brain may have collated in order for you to have these hunches. Was it using emotionally laden past experiences? Had it been influenced by subliminal advertising? Had it picked up diverse clues from a range of experiences?

129 Don't be too proud to fix other people's messes

Just because others may cause a problem and act irrespon-
sibly, this does not automatically rob you of your choice to
do something to rectify the situation. If it is in your interests
for it to be sorted, you don't have to wait around for them to
deal with it. Obviously, you may not wish to do this all the
time because then people will take advantage of you, but
from time to time you could do yourself a favour by getting
a quicker result.

130 Give your perfectionism a constructive outlet

It is quite likely that you are someone who is driven to do most things perfectly – most people with low self-esteem are. This can be one of the many reasons why their self-esteem is so low. Since perfection is rarely possible, you must find yourself continually disappointed with your results. When your confidence grows to a reasonable level, this problem should take care of itself because confident people are not afraid of making mistakes and do not need to please the whole world. But, in the meantime, you can lessen the pressure on yourself by channelling your perfectionism into particular outlets that hold high value to you. This will allow you to accept good-enough standards in other areas more readily. For example, you may choose to go for the very highest standards in the one specific area of your work that is noticed most by your superiors, and one aspect of your home life that involves caring for your children. You could work as much overtime as you need on the first and spend as much emotional energy on the second as you like.

Wandering concentration is a signal worth listening to. It may be telling you that you are bored and need more variety to stimulate you. It may be telling you that you are out of your depth and need more explanation or help. But more often than not it is probably just telling you that you need a break.

Next time your concentration wanders, resist giving yourself a hard time about it. Don't force yourself to keep going. Take a break. Even a few moments may do the trick, especially if you use those moments well (for instance, by doing a quick-fix relaxation or meditation).

133   Make a daily 'to do' list and monitor your results

Keep your daily lists for a month or two and see how you are achieving the everyday goals you set yourself. If you are regularly not achieving 100% success rate, then you are setting your sights too high. No wonder you don't feel good about yourself. Try making your lists more realistic.

134   Let yourself be disorganized sometimes

Although good personal organization is generally essential for making the best of our potential, we should sometimes allow ourselves a break. Not only does this give us a rest, but also when we let go of our routines, we give ourselves the opportunity to experience feelings we may not know we even had. Additionally, it is a well-known fact that creativity requires a certain amount of chaos in which to germinate its new ideas.

135 Don't expect decisions to make themselves magically

'Confident decision-making is an attainable goal that simply requires practice. There is no magic involved in making good decisions.'

ROGER DAWSON

136   Wait until you are calm before making a decision

Remember that the best decisions are rarely made when our system is tanked up to the brim with adrenalin – an overexcited state needs as much attention as a state of worry. Work on calming your body and mind.

137 Learn a strategy for making decisions

Here is one you can practise right now. You will need several sheets of paper, a pencil and an eraser. If possible, think of a real decision that you are currently struggling with. Alternatively, you could choose a hypothetical one that you fear you may have difficulty with in the future. Brainstorm all the different issues that are involved in this decision, such as money, health, self-esteem, job prospects, pleasing yourself and pleasing others. Divide another piece of paper into four columns. In the first column, list these issues – sifting out the least important. In the second column, enter a grading for each (perhaps on a scale of one to five) according to its current importance to you in terms of your needs. Next, grade them according to their feel-good factor (your heart, not your head, is the judge now). In the fourth column, enter a grading that is relevant to your long-term objectives and bigger life-goals. Now repeat all the above with the choices you have available. Compare and reflect on the sets of grades and make your decision. Now celebrate!

Try this simple exercise. It has helped many others to find parts of themselves they either had forgotten existed or never realized they had.

Take a large sheet of paper and write your name in the centre. Randomly jot down any words that come into your head when you think about you, such as thoughtful, shy, party-lover, gentle, loud and so on. In order to make full use of the creative side of your brain it is important not to censor ideas even if at the time they may seem silly or contradictory. If you allow yourself to free-associate you will automatically stimulate your creativity and will then be much more likely to produce information that the more logical, analytical side of your brain has forgotten or not noticed. (You will be able to edit out the irrelevant words later.) Leave the sheet of paper around for a few days, adding words as you observe yourself in action. Also, take some quiet time out to reflect back on scenes from your past life and add these to your sheet as well.

140 **View yourself as a team**

Using as a guide, the brainstorm you did of all the different aspects of you (see tip 138), choose 6–8 main title headings under which to organize these different aspects, (such as the organizer, the creator, the carer, the dogsbody, etc) Imagine that your 'team' had a new project to do (perhaps finding you a new job or accommodation). Give each a short description indicating the role they could play in helping you achieve your goal.

141 Write an advert for your inner team

Imagine that you have been given the task of selling your inner team's personal strengths to an organization such as a charity or small business. Write a short paragraph summarizing your inner team's strengths and potential.

142 Visualize your inner team working successfully together

This fun exercise requires you to be a little more creative. In your imagination, you give the different characteristics of your personality names and bodies (Brian the Boss; Nelson the Fighter; Archie the Artist, etc). Give them a task to perform and watch them in your mind's eye successfully completing this. You can use this exercise whenever you feel stuck and unable to think of a way forward with a problem.

143   Use past bad decisions to help you now

When you are stuck with a choice, think back to some decisions that you wish you had made differently. List down the wisdom you gained from these experiences and apply it to the choice you have now.

Our values are constantly modified without us realizing that they have been. We are all subject to mass media communication which has a powerful effect on the sub-conscious. You may enjoy watching soaps and violent movies, but do you want them to be guiding subconsciously the decisions you make in your life? You may also enjoy watching the TV ads and flicking through the advertisements in magazines, but do you really want your life to be run by commercially minded marketing gurus?

The best way to keep control of their influence is to remind yourself from time to time of the core values that you want to be guiding your life and then check your behaviour and choices against these. If you are a regular participant in religious services, you may already be doing this, but if not you will need to make a habit of doing this at other times (for example, while you are travelling home from work each Wednesday evening; or when you are in the sauna at the gym on Saturdays).

Try to match your external image with the inner you. Of course, you will have to be selective. The inner parts of you that you will want to externalize will be your best and not your worst. For example, if you are a creative person, ensure that your external appearance indicates that strength and that it doesn't just show that you are a slave to the current fashion. If you are an organized highly competent person, think twice about choosing an appearance that looks unkempt and scruffy, even if that is the current look most of your friends are adopting. Have the courage to show off your strengths to the outside world.

147 Keep yourself well groomed

Freshly washed hair and well-manicured nails help us feel better about ourselves. Make sure that you groom yourself for your pleasure as well as that of others. Even if you are spending a weekend on your own or are not going out anywhere special, don't let your grooming standards drop.

148   Challenge your perceptions

Watch, read and listen to things that that will extend your way of looking at the world. For example: join a book group and you will find that there are many ways of reading the same book; buy a magazine that you don't normally read; watch the news on a different TV channel.

You will feel so much better about yourself if you extend your horizons and shed some of your prejudices.

149 Limit yourself to one risk at any one time

This is the way you build up your courage and confidence. Experiment with small risks that are not too anxiety provoking. (For example, a change of hairstyle, doing an advanced driving course, changing jobs or joining a dating agency).

This is especially important if nobody else might have noticed your achievement. You may not feel that what you have done is worthy of a reward because everyone else in the world appears to do it so effortlessly. The psychological impact of rewards is immense. They reinforce the self-esteem we gained from successfully taking the risk. Think of them as bonus brownie points – you get extra self-esteem for merely giving yourself extra pleasure!

151   Give your left brain regular rests

Give yourself plenty of practice in switching off your left brain (that's the side that controls reasoning, language and communication, learning ability, maths skills, organization and logic) and allowing your creative, emotional brain to take over. This can be achieved through meditation; listening to emotional music or rhythmic natural sounds such as a rippling brook; doodling; or having a hot bath with a sensuous aroma in flickering candle light.

You can never be absolutely sure what tomorrow is going to bring for you. Life is full of surprises that we can never anticipate. But generally speaking many of our days are fairly predictable. When you are thinking about tomorrow, give an extra thought to what you could do differently which would make it a more satisfying day for you.

153   View your life as a movie

Imagine that a film company has been hired to make a film about you. They have been given an unlimited budget and total freedom on its style as well as the actors and director. They are just about to approach you for your advice, so note your spontaneous answers to the following questions:

★ Which type of film would you choose to reflect your own overall style? (Perhaps a documentary, blockbuster adventure, intellectual drama, grand opera, musical, comedy of manners or a cartoon.)
★ Which famous actor or actress would you choose to play you?
★ What would be the title and subtitle of the film?

Compose two sentences that summarize the essence of the film and that could be used to market it. Then (and this is the key question!) ask yourself if this is a movie you'd enjoy watching.

154   Remember it is not all your fault

'To be nobody-but-yourself – in a world which is doing its best, night and day, to make you everybody else – means to fight the hardest battle which any human being can fight; and never stop fighting.'

EE CUMMINGS

155　Don't hold back your opinions

When your self-esteem is high, you will find that you are automatically much more forthright. When it is low you probably kick yourself regularly after an event for not having said what you were thinking. Isn't it particularly frustrating to hear people coming out with good ideas and witty remarks that you know were in your mind long before they opened their mouths?

Holding back on your opinions may protect you from 'odd looks' and arguments, but it also deprives you of the applause and esteem of others when you deserve to have it. When you begin to bite your tongue, remind yourself that you need the applause and can easily recover from critical looks. Remember also that expressing your thoughts and receiving feedback on them is one important way of growing our potential. If our opinion is wrong or slightly misguided, it is almost always better in the long run to know this rather than not know.

You may find that sometimes the words coming out of your mouth are not the ones that you would like to hear or intended to say. This is because your emotions have had too much influence. One way of ensuring that this doesn't happen is to calm your nerves or frustration before opening your mouth. If you are practising relaxation regularly, this should be easy and quick to do. The moment you start taking a deep breath, or say in your mind one of your calming affirmations, your feelings will become easier to control.

157 Script your speech before you say something important

Scripting out in writing before speaking is one of the oldest tricks in the book. Use it when you want to make a complaint, ask for something that you are afraid may get refused or when you want your view to make a powerful impression. Don't be ashamed of needing to do this. Even the most brilliant orators and articulate politicians do this. The punchiest most memorable lines in speeches, poems and books are the hardest to write and they have usually been re-written and edited for many hours before they are delivered. Remember that the fewer words you use the more impact you often make.

Also, the simpler and more direct your message is, the easier it will be on the ear and therefore more welcome. The easiest way of all to script is on a computer because you can delete and re-write so easily. But if you do not have access to one, paper and pen will do just as well. Make sure you have both at the ready in your pocket or bag. You can always make an excuse to take yourself away from a scene for a few moments and write down and edit what you want to say.

Challenge your own rationalizations

How often do you find yourself giving what seems to be a logical explanation for not having done something you know you should have done? For example:

★ Arriving late and saying you haven't had enough time, when you know that if you had left earlier or been better organized you would have managed very easily.
★ Breaking your diet with a chocolate bar and saying you were 'starving' and needed food instantly, when you know that you were simply being weak-willed in the face of temptation.

Make a short list of the rationalizing statements you commonly use and read these aloud. It will then be much easier to hear them the next time you find yourself using them.

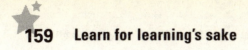

159   Learn for learning's sake

The feeling of achievement we gain from learning is a great self-esteem boost. Don't deny yourself this opportunity simply because you have no particular reason to extend your learning. For your psychological health, learning for learning's sake is good enough. So now you can give yourself permission to sign up for the adult education courses you have been denying yourself. It no longer matters that they seem like a 'luxury' or 'too wacky' – they are good for you!

160   Renew your New Year resolutions three times a year

This is the only way to ensure that you will keep them. Living with the knowledge that you cannot live up to your resolutions damages your self-esteem. Renewing them regularly gives you a chance to monitor and reward your progress. If you find that you are disappointing yourself, accept that you have set your sights too high. Modify your resolution so that it is much more achievable. Close your ears to *any* arguments to the contrary. To be told that your original resolutions should stay because they are easy 'if only you tried' does not help. Your self-esteem needs regular successes however small.

Select two other significant dates at a reasonable distance apart, such as your birthday, summer holiday or anniversary. Mark these in your diary as Resolution Review Days.

161   **Surround yourself with stimulation**

'To change yourself you first have to change your surroundings. A stimulating person lives and works in a stimulating environment, whilst a boring person lives and works in a boring environment.'

DAVID FREEMANTLE

162   Trust yourself to know when you are happy

Happiness is a subject that is now regularly debated in the public arena. Books on the subject are growing rapidly in number and some experts are even writing doctoral theses on the subject. For modern mortals, it seems that it is no longer enough to long for happiness, we have to be able to define, understand and work at it before we can hope to experience it!

People with high self-esteem don't have this problem. They don't look over their shoulders for guidance on this subject. They trust their own feelings. They don't need to fret about whether they are 'truly' happy – they know! They judge their current emotional state against others they have had in the past, rather than against hypothetical experiences others say they should or should not feel.

Trust that if you continue to be kind to yourself, respect your values and give yourself the life you deserve, you will experience happiness and you will know that you are doing so.

163 Get comfortable with solitude

Learn to be happy in your own company. If you are not used to intervals of solitude, start with very short periods. Try just ten minutes a day for the first two weeks. Expect to feel some negative feelings at first. These usually come from the child part of you that is frightened of loneliness (or the big bad wolf!). Do not chastise yourself for being 'silly' as this will only make the feelings worse. Instead, play the counsellor to your inner child. Try asking yourself questions to find out what your fear is about. For example, is it an out-of-date fear perhaps dating back from times in your childhood, or is it a more current one telling you that you have neglected your friends and family recently and they are beginning to reject you?

When you have discovered the reason, vow to do something positive to deal with the problem later and concentrate on making your solitude a pleasurable treat.

Have you ever had a great idea while standing in a queue somewhere or in the bath, and then cannot remember it later when later you want to share it? Accept that when your self-esteem is low, your memory isn't able to function as well as it normally can. Then jot down your ideas in a notebook or in a special file on your computer.

Quite commonly, people come back from their holiday jokingly saying, 'What I need now is a rest.' But not giving yourself the holiday you need is no joking matter. It is serious self-neglect.

Each of us needs something different from our holidays. Some of us need stimulation and fun from our summer break, while others need isolation and quiet. For a weekend break you may long for a quick infusion of a new culture to stimulate your mind, while others may be pining for a familiar comforting sofa.

Before your next holiday, use this checklist to ensure that you are planning to give yourself the break that *you* really want and need.

treats
relaxation
extra sleep
time to recharge mentally
nutritional boosts
stimulating change
opportunities to be myself
(not play roles)
time to 'remodel' myself
(new clothes, hairstyle,
fitter body, etc.)
relaxed time schedules
time to please myself

opportunities for daydreaming and fantasizing
fun
creative stimulation
freedom from emotional
restraint
chances to be looked after
choices to be with people I
like
experiences that bring me
back down to earth
time to reflect and reassess
goals

Put a copy of the list in your suitcase as a reminder to keep your promise to yourself.

168 Remember you are defeating yourself by not trying

'The deepest personal defeat suffered by human beings is constituted by the difference between what one was capable of becoming and what one has in fact become.'

ASHLEY MONTAGUE

Try to think of a success you have had in the past that deserved more celebration than it actually got. You must be able to find at least one, even if you have to dig deep into your memory bank. For example, you could choose:

★ A success at school that no one appreciated, perhaps because they didn't know how hard you had to try.
★ One that happened in a long series of tiny steps that seemed too insignificant to make much of – such as parenting a child.
★ One that was overlooked simply because there wasn't enough time to revel.

Celebrate it soon with at least one other person!

170 Give yourself a Diversion Day once in a while

Use one day of a weekend or take a day's leave to immerse yourself in your favourite pastime. Don't worry about whether your pastime is valuable or meaningful. It merely needs to give you pleasure and be able to take your mind off your worries. It doesn't matter if you choose to climb your nearest mountain or merely sit all day on the sofa watching football videos, as long as your Diversion Day works for you.

172 Distinguish the hard from the impossible

When you next hear yourself saying: 'Oh, but it is hard', repeat the following phrase which has helped so many others to gain perspective:

★ 'It may be hard but it is not impossible.'

173 Know who knows 95% of the real you

Not everyone needs to know every nook and cranny of your personality and past life. But your self-esteem will be bolstered in strength if you know that at least one or two people know and accept almost all of what there is to know about you. They don't necessarily need to be people who love you or live with you. They just need to be people who know the full picture and still genuinely respect you.

Ask yourself who you know who knows and accepts approximately 95% of the real you? If you cannot think of anyone, choose one or two people to whom you could risk revealing a little more of yourself. You may be in for some very pleasant surprises. The vast majority of people are very understanding of others' faults and past misjudgements. After all, human frailty is normal.

If you cannot think of anyone with whom to share yourself more, think about getting some counselling or therapy. This will at least give you a taste of this experience – even if you do have to pay for it. Alternatively, join a self-help group which should give it to you for free!

174   Acknowledge the power of your emotional wounds

These are past experiences which still trigger hurt or angry feelings when they are consciously or unconsciously recalled. We need to be fully aware of them because they can stop you from being fully the person you want to be or having the life you deserve. For example:

★ Dad's inability to express any feelings except anger has left me wary and resentful of this emotion.
★ Mum's moans about having to work, and the constant quarrels over who should do what at home left me cynical about the possibility of combining a career and motherhood.
★ The extreme poverty of the neighbourhood in which I lived left me feeling guilty about indulging in any luxury.
★ My sheltered and over-protected childhood didn't prepare me for the real world.

Once acknowledged they can at least be controlled, even if they can never be fully healed.

175   Keep a very private diary

You do not have to make a daily entry of your innermost thoughts, but try to ensure that you write them up at least three times a week. Then read it back to yourself every month or two. This will help you to become more self-aware and see the patterns that are guiding your thoughts and behaviour. It will also make you realize how much or how little progress you are making in building your self-esteem.

Make sure your diary is kept under lock and key. Also, take care not to write as though it were going to be read by anyone else but you. You are not writing for posterity or publication. This is a personal growth exercise which needs to be very personal and private.

177 Exercise your right brain regularly

Improve your creative potential by stimulating and exercising the right side of your brain. Here are some ideas:

★ deep-relaxation techniques to encourage daydreaming;
★ practise meditation;
★ listen to more music (without analyzing it);
★ allow yourself to doodle;
★ join in imaginative play with children;
★ improvisation games such as charades or Pictionary with adults;
★ make up rather than read stories for children;
★ use mind maps and brainstorms for making notes.

178 Use your dreams to understand your needs

Not every dream is significant, but the recurring and emotionally haunting ones usually are. It is worth taking a short time each morning to check out if your dreaming has any message for you.

On waking, talk yourself through your dream again as though it were happening in the present. If the dream felt unfinished, imagine an ending. Take special note of the feelings and powerful images. Remembering that dream feelings often relate to those we are trying to deny and that dream images are often metaphors for parts of ourselves, try to make some connection with the major issues and internal conflicts that are going on in your life. Note down what action you are going to take; for example, 'Make a decision about …' or 'Talk to him about …'

179 Write and recite your own Credo

Credos are used by religions because they are very effective at establishing beliefs in our mind. They are a kind of positive brainwashing. Often they are recited to music. You can use this principle to establish good beliefs about yourself in your mind.

Complete the sentence, 'I believe ...' as many times as you can, as in these following examples.

★ 'I believe that I am an exciting and unique person with loads of potential.'
★ 'I believe that I can be assertive and powerful.'
★ 'I believe that I can love and be loved.'
★ 'I believe that the environment can be preserved.'
★ 'I believe that there are alternatives to war.'
★ 'I believe that people can change for the better as well as for the worse.'
★ 'I believe that I can be successful at work.'

Put on some music that is both enjoyable and calming. (It helps if it has a regular beat.) Recite your beliefs over and over again.

If you cannot control the dangers and risks you have to face, remember that you *can* control your reaction to them. This is an area where mind very obviously can triumph over matter. We do not have to be our body's slave. We can control the paralysing effects of fear, but only if first we take responsibility for our own feeling.

When you hear yourself saying something like 'It was too frightening', change your statement to 'I was too frightened' or 'I allowed myself to get too paralysed by my fear.'

181 Identify the root triggers to your persistent fears

Use this exercise to help you understand how a fear from the past or an unmet current emotional need may be making you more fearful than you need to be.

List 10 of your recurring fears, including some big ones and some little ones. Note, as in the example below, the common current triggers for each and a possible underlying root trigger that may be increasing your fear.

Fear	Current Triggers	Root Causes
Being lonely	Someone is late	I spent too much time on my own as a kid
Large cities	I don't like my own company	Arguments with friends
Ageing	Seeing grey hairs	My mother died young
Being ill	Financial insecurity	I'm not very fit

Next time you feel the fear, remind yourself of your root trigger. This will help you to get the fear into a manageable proportion. (If it is at all possible, you should also take action to deal with the root causes.)

If this sounds a very sacrilegious exercise, remember that you don't have to show it to anyone and you are doing it for a good reason. You are not setting out to create a new religion!

Write down a list of ten 'should' statements for yourself (for example, 'I should be honest'), then put them in hierarchical order with what you see as the most important commandment as No. 1.

Pin these up in your home somewhere and monitor your behaviour in relation to this list from time to time.

183 Treat each minor loss as a mini-bereavement

If you find you can't pull yourself together as quickly as others seem to be able to after a small loss (such as losing or being robbed of a favourite object), it could be that you are not grieving properly. Many people with low self-esteem didn't learn how to look after themselves emotionally during their childhood years. You could be piling up a store of unresolved grief deep within you that gets re-triggered with each new minor loss. Each time you have a small loss, allow yourself to go through the following natural emotional stages.

1　**Shock** – feeling frozen, unable to move or feel anything.
2　**Denial** – acting as though it hadn't happened; carrying on doing what you were doing before the loss.
3　**Depression** – feeling hopeless about the loss; being convinced that you will never recover and that you cannot do without what you have lost; mourning your loss through crying.
4　**Anxiety** – worrying about whether you will lose something else.
5　**Anger** – feeling angry with the person or situation you believe caused your loss.
6　**Acceptance** – realizing that you have to move on in spite of your loss; taking responsibility for finding compensation for your loss; acknowledging the true (and unexaggerated) impact of the consequences of your loss.

Remember that with a very minor loss this process may only take a matter of minutes as compared with a couple of years for major bereavements. The healing process should progress through exactly the same stages whatever the loss.

Very commonly, people with low self-esteem don't like to ask for comfort, or indeed any other kind of help when they are 'bereaved'. This is because most were not sufficiently encouraged or able to lean on others for support after losses during their childhood. Alternatively, when you tried, you were rejected or your cry for help was not noticed.

Do you have memories of being told to pull yourself together and stop crying when all you needed was a cuddle? Do you recall being told that you shouldn't feel upset or angry when you began to talk about how you were feeling? Do you recall thinking that your parents or teachers were themselves too busy, worried or upset to help? Were you convinced that the adults around you thought you were being childish to be so upset over such a minor thing? Were you too busy helping others who were upset to give your own feelings much space? If so, resolve to give yourself more practice at sharing and taking comfort. You might make resolutions similar to these:

★ Talk to a friend about the bitterness I feel over my divorce and how this is stopping me from looking twice at potential new partners.
★ Next time I have a loss, instead of putting a brave face on it, seek out a friend with whom I can cry quite openly because I have spent too much of my life being strong and brave.
★ When I feel I am losing my looks, instead of telling myself to stop being so vain, I will share my thoughts with friends of the same age and suggest we share an indulgence together as compensation.

185 Deal openly with jealousy

Low self-esteem and the conviction of being 'second rate' are the root cause of persistent jealousy. Don't make matters worse today by nursing these feelings inside of you and feeling ashamed of them.

Have the courage to discuss your feelings with the person concerned. But make sure that you take full responsibility for your feelings and don't accuse that person of making you jealous. (Even if they have been goading you.) Say something which simply acknowledges the problem is yours and that you are dealing with it. (And, yes you are. You are building up your self-esteem right now.) Finally, remember there is no need to include a put-down – of you or them. A simple statement like the ones below will build your self-respect and earn respect from others. (The goaders will stop goading when they realize you are not going to rise to their bait.) For example:

★ 'When I see you looking so handsome and others looking admiringly at you, I feel jealous. I know that I have to deal with this feeling myself and am doing my best to do so.'
★ 'Each time your ex rings and you seem to be having a friendly exchange about the past or your children, I go green. I don't like this jealous response of mine and will leave the room when she rings until I have learned to deal with it better.'

How often have you bought clothes and other items, simply because you were tired and fed-up with looking around and being unable to choose? Then, the next morning you wake up and look at your purchases and think how stupid you have been.

The truth is that often you have made bad purchases because you became angry and fed-up with yourself for being so indecisive. You have given yourself a double punishment.

Next time you find yourself in that position, stop shopping. Pause for a coffee or 'sleep on it' before buying. Think through once again the pros and cons of what you have seen so far and make up your mind what you are going to buy before you return to the shops. Then treat yourself to a reward. This way you will have boosted rather than booted your self-esteem!

187 Say 'No' simply, firmly and directly

Don't hint or beat about the bush. Don't offer any unnecessary excuses. If you don't want to do something, say directly that you don't rather than biting your lip and doing it resentfully. Use a strong firm tone of voice, looking the other person straight in the eye.

This kind of assertive behaviour offers no guarantee, but it will substantially increase your chances of your view being noticed and respected. Sometimes, you may still have to do what someone else wants, however directly and firmly you say 'no'. But at least your self-esteem won't suffer. You will feel proud of yourself for making your stand.

188 Save for the leisure and pleasure you deserve

It is not fair to yourself to deny yourself treats just because you have not saved carefully enough. Aim to have at least two or three affordable treats planned for well into the future. Then start separate named savings schemes for each one (for instance, 40th Birthday; Summer holiday; Christmas show; Olympic ticket). That will help you think twice before dipping into the funds for other reasons and ensure that you budget fairly and wisely.

189   Treat problems like jigsaws

When you feel overwhelmed, try approaching solving your problem in the way you would tackle a jigsaw.

1   Lay all the pieces out in a jumble form – you can do this by writing out different aspects of your problems and feelings on small pieces of paper. Write them out as soon as they come into your head, working very fast without thinking too hard (as you would in a brainstorm session).
2   Group similar 'pieces' together – you could, for example, put all the feelings together or the financial aspect or the organizational aspects or the impact on others.

You will notice that immediately you feel more in control and confident than by attempting to solve it piece by piece. (Don't all jigsaws look impossible when they are first tipped out of their box?)

190 **Take regular breaks when problem-solving**

Once you are in the throes of solving a problem it is sometimes very tempting to 'soldier on' until it is solved. This is particularly true for people who haven't much confidence in themselves. They are afraid that if they stop they will not be able to re-start or that they may be seen as weak for needing a break.

Remind yourself that you cannot give of your best when you are tired and then force yourself to stop to re-charge your energy at frequent intervals. Set an alarm to remind you that your break is due.

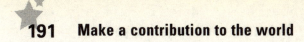

191   Make a contribution to the world

Choose a universal cause to support such as global warming or pollution and make an anonymous contribution. This could be giving a donation of money or changing a habit that will help the cause.

By keeping your contribution secret, you will know that you are doing it for you and the world, not to impress others.

192 Think before delegating your difficulties

Of course, it is good to delegate sometimes. Others may be *very* much more able to do the job, or you may simply have too much to do. But how often do you automatically rush to someone else before you have given yourself the opportunity to solve a problem yourself. When our self-esteem is low we have a tendency to delegate too quickly and often. Don't deprive yourself of the satisfaction of achievement or even a good attempt.

193 Watch out for double standards

When you are beating yourself up about something, ask yourself if you would do the same to someone whom you love for the same offence. If the answer is 'no' (and it usually is), ask yourself why you are practising double standards?

PART 3

RELATIONSHIPS

195　Think before you question

You probably don't rate yourself very highly as a conversationalist. This may be because you always feel the other person is in control and leading the way. Having just a small amount of knowledge about the way questioning works will help you to feel more empowered and get more of what you want out of conversations.

The words you use to phrase your question can determine the kind of answer you receive and how long the conversation may last. These are two main types of questions:

1　Open – the kind of questions which are most likely to give you more than a 'yes' or 'no' answer. They often start with the words 'How', 'When', 'Where', 'What', 'Who' or 'Why'.
2　Closed – the kinds of questions that limit the options for the other person. They usually lead to a 'yes' or 'no' answer or a limited choice response. They often begin with the words 'Do you', 'Did you', 'Would you', 'Will you' or 'Which would you …'.

Use open-ended questions if you want to keep a conversation going or need to gather more or more specific information. Use closed questions if you want to round things up or get a decision or definite opinion from someone.

Time doesn't necessarily do this work for you. You need to check that you are doing the following, if you want to keep these relationships especially intimate and very supportive:

★ Make sure that you have quality time together so you can talk without being interrupted or distracted.
★ Share your thoughts and feelings openly about 90 per cent of the time (it is OK and good to have some secrets).
★ Show respect for the other person's right to hold back from sharing if they choose to do so.
★ Keep having fun together – even if you do not have time to do much else.

You need to check that your relationship is changing and developing to meet the current needs and expectations of both parties. One of the main reasons for break-ups and misunderstandings is that the patterns in a relationship have become stuck even though the people in them are moving on. You might recognize these common examples:

★ A dad who keeps treating his daughter like a little girl and the daughter dutifully responding in a childlike manner.
★ The husband who continues to be overly protective, long after his wife's pregnancy.
★ The colleague who is too familiar with someone who has been promoted several rungs on the ladder above them.
★ The single friend who expects her married mother of five to be available as a listening ear 24 hours a day like she was in her teens.

If you are not getting what you want or are no longer able to give the other person what they now need, be assertive and say so. Your self-esteem will suffer if you feel inadequate or misunderstood as a friend.

198 Agree with the truth in criticisms

This is a technique that is taught in assertiveness training classes. It is not as easy as it sounds, because you may think you are making yourself more vulnerable. In fact, you are doing the opposite. You are protecting yourself. The reason is that when you calmly agree with the truth, or the element of truth in a criticism, the average critic is usually taken aback and will not say anything more. An aggressive bully will not be deterred by this technique and then you need to use different tactics (see tip 338).

Even if you have done wrong or made a mistake, not everyone needs to hear your mitigating circumstances. Indeed, you may irritate them further by attempting to explain the reason for your mistake or fault. Watch confident people take fair criticism. Very frequently, they will just admit their fault and apologize for it. They will not add an explanation.

For example: 'Yes, I know I did that badly, I'm sorry', then adding '... but I was pushed for time' would probably invite further criticism. Sometimes it may be appropriate to defend yourself (for example, in response to a criticism at work), but it is rarely a good idea to do this during or in the aftermath of a mistake. It is usually better to defend yourself later when you are calm and have thought through what you need to say or request to help you avoid making the same mistake again.

200 Don't give yourself a put-down in response to a justified criticism

This is a common habit in unassertive people, but one you should try hard to break. All you need to do is agree with the criticism. You can also add an apology and say what you are going to do to right the wrong when it is appropriate to do so. But you do not need to do a character assassination on yourself as well. Here are some examples which might ring some bells. The unnecessary put-down is highlighted:

A: 'This desk is a complete tip. You're hopelessly disorganized.'
B: 'Yes, it's true. I'm not very tidy. I'm sorry I will tidy it now. **I'm impossible – always creating more work for myself.**'

A: 'You've put on a good deal of weight since we last met.'
B: 'Yes I have. **I look disgusting.**'

202 Spend more time with young children

They will not mind your imperfections and are more likely to accept and love you for what you are. They will give you a reminder of how bonding spontaneity and fun can be. Even if you do not have any young children of your own, you could offer yourself as a babysitter or play companion to close friends and relatives.

203 Release your tension before a confrontation

When you are in a position of having to work or live with people who continually take advantage of your goodwill, resources, time or space, your body will inevitably be put under strain. Before taking steps to deal with the relationship issues, ensure that you release your physical tension safely. Unless you do this, you may well find that your tension causes you to behave and speak in ways that you may later regret.

204 Worry less about what insignificant others think

How many times do you hold back from saying, doing or wearing what you want, just because of what other people who are not known to you may think? Make a conscious effort not to do this when you are next on holiday or are in a place where the people around are strangers (and likely to remain so). Give yourself the freedom to experiment with being spontaneous and even eccentric.

205 Deal with mini-frustrations promptly

This is a great general rule for every kind of relationship, but it is the golden key to managing essential difficult relationships. However, it is also one of those obvious rules that we know but often don't follow. We don't tell our partner (yet again!) to pick up their socks or tights from the bedroom floor because we don't want to be seen as a nag. Then we reach our threshold of built-up tension and throw our frustration at them in a tirade of overly hurtful and unnecessary abuse. If your relationship is strong it can withstand occasional outbursts, but if it is basically rocky, then they can be disastrous. So, if you have to live or work with people you do not relate to easily, make sure that you only ever sweep your frustration under the carpet in emergency situations.

206 Test the depth of your relationships with your faults

Not all your friends have to love you 'warts and all', but it helps to be clear about who does. Knowing this can help you to avoid being hurt and rejected. You can choose to avoid showing the sides of you that may not be accepted by some people. For example, if you tend to be indecisive and you know this trait drives one friend mad, you can let them or others do the choosing when you are with them. Try this exercise.

Make a list of the key adult relationships you currently have in your life. Then write down six of your worst faults. Who among these people knows about these faults? If they do know or were to find out, how do (or might) they react to them? Are they demanding (or would they demand) that you change them? Do you think they will (or would) continue to love you even if you did not change them?

207   **Use friends with a sense of humour to keep perspective**

The day he moved out was terrible.
That evening she went through hell.
His absence wasn't the problem,
but the corkscrew had gone as well.

WENDY COPE

208 Don't be afraid of looking back after a rejection

In the immediate aftermath of a traumatic rejection, you may find yourself acting as though it had never happened. This is natural and it is healing. Denial works to protect you from unmanageable pain in the short term. It gives your body some breathing space to recover from the shock. But at some point, you have to face what has happened if you want to heal fully and move on with your life.

If you find you resist looking back because you cannot face the pain again, you may have to encourage yourself to do so. If you have a close friend you can do this with, so much the better. Set aside some quiet uninterrupted time to talk over or replay significant scenes from the relationship in your mind. Use photographs or symbolic objects, such as presents from your loved one, to recapture the memories. Play music that you associate with special times, and let the painful memories surface.

Don't pretend that you are stronger or less hurt than you really are. There is no shame in being rejected – it happens to the most beautiful, talented and confident people as well. You need, just as they do, to express your feelings. If you don't, your health could suffer as a result of unreleased tension. So give yourself some private time and space to let go of whatever feelings need to be released. Let the tears flow or thump a cushion if you feel angry. Try not to judge your feelings or let anyone else judge them as they emerge. Very often we are surprised by our feelings – we may feel anger when we thought we should be sad or vice versa. If you can't express either physically, try writing about what happened. It is important not to worry about *how* you write – just let your mind and pen wander and don't hold back with your language. These notes can be shredded later. Alternatively, write a never-to-be-posted letter to your ex.

211   Let yourself be comforted by others after a rejection

You may feel awkward taking comfort. Your low self-esteem may make you think you don't deserve it. You may be telling yourself that you were stupid to get into this relationship. Maybe you were and maybe you weren't – you can judge that later when you are emotionally stronger and your self-esteem has been repaired. Remind yourself that allowing yourself to be comforted and looked after is an important stage in the emotional healing process. Find a caring, non-judgmental friend who is willing to hug you – either literally or metaphorically. Remember physical comfort is not everyone's style. Don't think you are being rejected yet again if your comforter doesn't do cuddles. Having a cup of warming tea or a pint of refreshing beer bought for you can be equally healing.

Receiving compensation after being disappointed is an essential part of the emotional healing process. It is also a very natural one. A good parent automatically gives their child a compensatory treat after a much-loved toy has been broken or taken away. When we become adults we should naturally start to do this for ourselves. But people with low self-esteem rarely do – you may have to force yourself into taking a little compensation. You could take yourself to somewhere you have always wanted to go, but your ex wouldn't have liked. Or, now that there is only you to cook for, you could indulge yourself with a luxury meal. Alternatively, you could treat yourself to a small present. It doesn't have to be expensive –you are buying it for its symbolic significance more than anything else. Choose an object you can keep in a place where you will see it every-day or something that you can wear frequently.

213 Help yourself gain a new perspective after a rejection

The emotional state of grief can warp our sense of perspective about our potential and ourselves. We tend to see ourselves as much weaker and less attractive than we really are. To counter these feelings, remind yourself of your achievements and strengths, and also the wisdom you acquired as a result of being in this relationship and having this rejection. If you find this very difficult to do, talk to a friend who you know has made a good recovery from a broken heart. Ask them what they learned and just see how quickly and positively they respond. Trust that you will soon start thinking like them.

A break-up may reveal just how dependent you were on your ex. Don't cut yourself up about having been so dependent (it happens naturally when our self-esteem is low). Instead, vow not to let it happen again. In the best relationships, both parties are emotionally self-reliant. See this as a great opportunity to build up your sense of inner independence. Take yourself to places that you know you will enjoy and where you will see other people being happy on their own. For example, this could be a gallery, museum or café in a large bustling city, or it could be a holiday or hotel that specializes in packages for single people. This will help you to associate being on your own with pleasure. Try to avoid pairing up immediately – even if an attractive offer comes your way. Your loneliness will pass, but you could make an unwise choice while you are still at its mercy. Remind yourself that it will pay long-term dividends to have time to develop more self-reliance. (And, of course, you can always ask for the address or phone number of that tempting other and contact them later!)

215 Empower others to reveal their preferences

When our self-esteem is low, we often cannot imagine that people may find it difficult to speak their mind with us. But for a whole variety of reasons this may be the case. For example, we may be very impressive externally in spite of our inner wobbliness, or the other person could be even wobblier inside than we are. Empowering them to be more forthright with you will make you feel good and strengthen your relationship.

Make it easy for people to express their opinions and needs by suggesting alternatives. For example, instead of asking 'What do you want to do tonight?', give them some choices. You could say, 'I was thinking that there are several things we could do tonight and can't decide. We could go to the cinema or a restaurant, or just stay in with a takeaway. Which would you prefer?'

217 Make sure that your positive friends outnumber the moaners

You can't avoid being with negative friends sometimes. You may have some that you are very close to, in spite of their moans and groans. But negativity is very catching and while your self-esteem is low, you must protect yourself from it as much as you can. Every so often do a spot-check on your friendships in terms of how they make you feel. It may be time to correct the balance and seek out the company of more people who help you to feel uplifted.

218 Know what you expect from a friendship before you foster it

Do this exercise on your own at first, then share it later with your new friend and see if their expectations match yours. If they don't, be aware that you are in for trouble!

Complete the following two sentences as many times as you can without thinking too long and hard before writing.

★ 'I believe relationships work best when …'
(For example: '… the two people respect each other'; '… are different to each other'; '… make each other the first priority'; '… are not too dependent on each other'.)

★ 'I'd hate to be in a relationship …'
(For example: '… where one person is more dominant than the other'; '… which is safe but boring'; '… where you lived in each other's pockets'.)

You can set the tone for the future of your relationship during your first hour of meeting. If you begin by sharing all the awful things that have happened to you in your life, that is what you may get forever after. Try getting to know someone by asking them about the best times in their lives.

221   Improve your listening skills

An ability to listen well can make you a very attractive friend. (And, in the long run, it may keep you being attractive long after your other charms may have worn thin.) The key to being able to listen well is not endless sympathetic patience, but active participation. Here are some tips to help you improve your listening skills.

★ Hold back on interrupting with your 'story'(for example, 'Oh, the same thing happened to me when …').

★ If you are talking face-to-face, try to maintain direct eye contact about 50% of the time. Never stare.

★ Match the other person's tone of voice. If they speak quietly, lower your tone.

★ Use plenty of nods and encouraging words to let them know you are still listening.

★ Repeat back the end of their last sentence to encourage them to continue talking.

★ Ask open rather than closed questions to get them to clarify and expand on what they are saying (see tip 195).

★ Use their name occasionally when asking a question or making a comment.

★ Check that you have understood their feelings accurately (for example, 'I notice you looked worried when you said that …, are you?').

Drawing a pie chart is a very quick and easy way to do this. Look at your diary over the last 6 months and calculate how much of your leisure time has been with, for example, old friends, making new friends, having fun, serious chat, sharing activities, etc. Draw a pie chart giving each an appropriately sized section. Study it and ask yourself if you are getting the balance right. Decide what you may need to do differently to ensure you meet your real social needs.

224 Don't credit luck with your successes

Take pride in the good relationships you have chosen and built. Don't give away the credit of your successes to luck. When part of you or someone else says, for example, 'You're so lucky to have found such a brilliant friend', don't reply 'I know.' Remind yourself that you chose your friend and contributed to the relationship.

The main technique used in assertiveness training is called 'broken record'. This is the self-protective skill of being able to repeat over and over again, in an assertive and relaxed manner, what it is you want and need until the other person gives in or agrees to negotiate with you. It helps you to persist in asserting your feelings, opinions or wishes, whatever pressure the other person may put you under. Here's an example:

Unexpectedly, Jack had to drive someone to hospital one evening after work. His wife Jill expected him home, but Jack's mobile battery was flat so he could not contact her. After dropping the person at hospital, he drove straight home and tried to tell Jill his story, but she kept interrupting. He uses the broken record technique to persuade her to let him explain.

> Jack: *Just as I was leaving the office …*
> Jill: *That's what you always say. I've been here up to my eyes …*
> Jack: *Let me explain please …*
> Jill: *It's just an excuse. You just don't care about …*
> Jack: *Jill, let me explain.*
> Jill: *I've heard it before. You …*
> Jack: *I want to explain.*
> Jill: *Okay then.*
> Jack: *As I was leaving the office …*

The more you practise your assertive responses, the more likely they will automatically appear just when you need them. This is particularly important when it comes to criticism. The less assertive we are in our responses, the more criticism we are likely to receive – and no one with low self-esteem needs that! Try this exercise now.

1 List some of the criticisms you have had in the past that you have not liked hearing.
2 Add some that you may not have yet heard, but would not be pleased to hear.
3 Beside each, write down an assertive, polite response. This could simply be an acknowledgement that the criticism is true, or that it *might* be true. Alternatively, it could be a polite denial such as 'I accept that you believe I have not done my best but I assure you that I have.'
4 Practise saying your responses several times in front of a mirror using a calm, steady voice, an upright posture and direct eye contact. Doing this will help you to be more controlled and confident next time you hear this criticism or a similar one.

227 Be more generous with your compliments

Almost certainly you do not give as many compliments as you could give or even want to give. You probably hold back, not wanting to appear cheeky, forward or patronizing. You may not give enough value to your compliment either, thinking that the other person may not be that impressed because it is 'only' from you. Or you might just be too timid to open your mouth.

One way of increasing your rate of compliment giving is to prepare for it. Think ahead and practise what you want to say so that you don't become tongue-tied when you approach the person. Try first with a good friend. There is always something more that we can say to our friends that they would like to hear.

Compliments feed the self-esteem of both the giver and the receiver. An additional motivator to remember is that the more you give the more you are likely to receive.

228 Don't include a self put-down when giving a compliment

This is a common bad habit, so watch for it in yourself. It masquerades as humility, but rarely has anything to do with that noble quality. It is usually either a way of coping with embarrassment or a strategy to draw attention to our own neediness. It is self-destructive behaviour because it often embarrasses the other person and annoys them, making them feel manipulated into rescuing you with a compliment or reassurance. Here are some examples (the self put-downs are in bold):

★ 'Thank you so much for helping me. You are always so kind. **I wish I was as thoughtful as you.**'
★ 'I love that coat on you. **That style would make me look even more enormous than I already am.**'

229   Avoid gossipers and backbiting

It is very tempting to join in a secret gossip or moan session about difficult people behind their backs. It can seem like harmless fun and feel comforting, but it can also be damaging for our self-esteem. You have to be a hard, aggressive person to feel good about putting others down behind their backs.

230 Don't encourage others to tell you how you feel

It is likely that there are several people in your life who might claim to know you better than yourself. This is quite a common problem for people with low self-esteem. In fact, they often encourage this 'arrogance' by asking too readily for others' opinions. Here are some examples that might sound familiar:

★ 'Do you think I'm really in love with him, or am I just flattered by his attention?'
★ 'Would I get too frightened if I tried that?'
★ 'Do you think I'll be disappointed if I go to see that film?'
★ 'Will I just get more jealous and possessive, if I stop going to parties with her?'

232 Remember, if you are angry you could be irrational

This means that you could say or do something that you would later feel ashamed about and might lower your esteem in others' eyes. If you feel angry:

★ Stop and get some distance from the person or situation;
★ Release your physical tension safely;
★ Breathe slowly;
★ Compose a script before you speak, checking that it is polite and assertive.

233   Smile with your eyes

Weak smiles are embarrassing to give and to receive. You don't necessarily always have to broaden your mouth to its extremes to give a strong smile. In many circumstances, it is more appropriate and appealing to use your eyes to make a confident impact.

234 Maintain your dignity when treated rudely

Don't add injury to insult. You will hurt your self-esteem if you react to bad manners in a way that diminishes you in the eyes of others or yourself. When you feel 'piqued' by rude or inconsiderate behaviour, take three deep breaths and remind yourself to stay in control. In a calm assertive voice and making direct eye contact with the person, say that you did not like being treated in that manner or state how you would prefer to be treated (for instance, 'I don't like it when you raise your voice. I would prefer you not to swear or interrupt me when I have just started talking.').

Resist the temptation to lecture or insult the other person. ('You should ...' or 'People like you should ...') Also, don't threaten them with a 'punishment' when it is obvious that you cannot or will not follow through. ('I'll never speak to you again.'; 'I'll make sure the directors hear about this.'; or 'I'll kill you.')

235 Script and edit your requests

Prepare your 'speech' in writing. You can then edit it to ensure that it is:

★ Concise and doesn't include any unnecessary words or justifications or apologies;
★ Uses objective and simple language rather than manipulative emotional pleas and unnecessary jargon;
★ Indicates consideration for others' needs, problems and feelings;
★ States plainly and directly what you want;
★ Points out the benefits to the other party.

This does not mean that you have to adopt a cocky arrogant tone, merely a positive, confident upbeat one. Convince yourself before you speak that you have a right to ask, even if there is a chance that you will be refused. (Don't ask unless you believe this to be true, otherwise your self-esteem may be harmed.)

237 Make a habit of telling people your good news

Many people with low self-esteem are reluctant to do this. They tell themselves that their news is not very significant in the eyes of others; or that they are worried about making people feel envious or upset because their life is not so good at the moment. The reality is that the vast majority of people love hearing about other people's pleasurable experiences and successes, even when they are feeling low themselves. Positive feelings are just as contagious as negative ones and you will be more likely to uplift others rather than depress them. Of course, it is important not to use bragging language or an overly rousing tone – but then the chances of someone with low self-esteem doing this are highly remote, aren't they?!

238 Keep reminders of others' special days

Accept that when your self-esteem is low, your memory is not always as good as it could be. Mark dates in your diary to help you avoid feeling bad about forgetting to congratulate people on birthdays and wish them luck for difficult challenges.

This is an alternative to avoiding situations and people that make you angry. (Yet another of those annoying low self-esteem habits!)

Write down a list of phrases or 'looks' that you know are likely to irritate or inflame you. Compose a polite assertive response to each. Then take yourself into a deeply relaxed state (in the bath would do). Close your eyes and visualize a scene that you have prepared for. Watch yourself responding in a calm controlled but self-protective manner. The more often you do this, the less fearful you will be of these situations and people.

Fake confidence until you feel it

This is a trick that may not work 100% of the time, but it is certainly worth giving it a go, rather than avoiding people who make you tremble. The reason it works is that you will receive more respect from others as a result. You are more likely to be noticed, heard and appreciated. This may not be fair or just, but it is reality. You know that you feel more at ease around people who appear confident and in control. Confidence inspires trust – even when it is faked!

241 Know when and when not to use advice-givers

It wouldn't be surprising if most of your current friends come into this category! If so, you are probably not getting good advice or getting the kind of support that you need to build your self-esteem.

Advice-givers are great when we need information that we are unable to access ourselves or if we are in a state of shock and unable to think for ourselves. They are not so great in situations where they are called upon to help with personal dilemmas. In these situations, all you need is a good listener. (Many hairdressers and taxi drivers would qualify!) An advice-giver (even the professional kind) is likely to be much too subjective and directive in this kind of situation. As counsellors are only too well aware, when most people have a personal dilemma they know what they need to do. All they need is someone to listen attentively to them until they have plucked up the courage to do what they need or want to do.

Unless you need a 'white lie' to protect your privacy, tell the truth. It usually works more effectively and leaves you feeling better about yourself. Think twice about being dishonest to protect someone's feelings. If you are found out, this could be perceived as patronizing, so you will have defeated your purpose. If you are not found out, you could be asked again and again until you become irritated and show your feelings.

243   Use tricks to remember names

Your anxiety on meeting new people may make recalling their names especially difficult. One trick is to use their name at least three times in the immediate conversation. Another is to ask for their card, say their name as you read it and then ask a question about it. A third one is on hearing their name, to try and link it to an object or another person you can visualize. For example 'John Linden – isn't Linden the name of a tree?' or 'Jill Marley – sister of the famous Bob, I assume?!'

There are many, many more tricks you can learn. Ask colleagues and friends for their favourites and then try each until you find the one that works for you.

244 Practise enjoying praise

Use creative visualization to overcome any embarrassment you feel over accepting praise or recognition from others. Take yourself into a physically relaxed state and use your imagination to conjure up pictures of yourself calmly taking deserved praise and rewards from others.

Does this sound unkind? It probably does to you – but is it? The truth is that many of these friendships are making matters worse for both parties. Think seriously about how much energy and time you can give to others who are in a needy emotional state. The fact that you can understand their plight better than most may not be a good enough reason to befriend them. They might be better off spending more time with people who don't understand but still inspire them – and so could you!

246 Use scintillating small talk to protect yourself

Being able to talk superficially with an air of confidence and energy is a great skill. It is also an essential one for people with low self-esteem. It gives us a breathing space to gain trust in the other person before we take the relationship forward onto a more personal level.

Before going into a situation where you know you will meet new people, prepare your small talk. Get up to date with the latest news, but be careful not to express your views on it unless it is a neutral subject. (Avoid politics and religious issues, of course.) Don't be afraid to talk about weather, but do try to think of an interesting statistic or unusual experience. Ideally, think of something that may interest the other people. For example, perhaps you find some interesting fact or story on the internet about the building they are working in or the town in which they live. One of the best small-talk tricks is to try to link the subject to something you know a good deal about, but most people don't, or encourage the other person to climb onto their hobby horse.

It is demeaning for you and rarely endears you to the recipient. If you overdo adulation and compliance, most successful people become suspicious that perhaps they are being emotionally manipulated – even if that is far from your intention. The truth is that if you want to impress successful and confident people, you have to appear confident and successful yourself. This does not mean that you have to excel academically, or be rich or powerful. You merely have to show that you are good at doing what you do well and have dealt with the challenges that have come your way in a positive manner.

Remember that the successful people worth knowing (the ones that may help you) do not get their buzz from admiration, they get it from achievement and helping others to achieve.

Be aware of hidden manipulative bait

You probably don't need to be told that some people take advantage of those with low self-esteem and an eagerness to please. But be aware that they often dress up their manipulation in sheep's clothing. Be on the look out for flattering bait.

★ 'I know they'll be so disappointed.' (*Bait:* they will not like you.)

★ 'Everyone who is anyone is going to be there – do come with me.' (*Bait:* you'll lose status if you don't.)

★ 'Oh, go on do it. Be an angel. I am so stressed out at the moment.' (*Bait:* you'll go to heaven if you rescue me.)

250 Play safe with self-disclosure

Self-disclosure can bring you closer to people, but it can also make some good and interesting people run a mile and never return. This is not necessarily because of what you said, but when you said it. It is most likely that you went too deep too soon. Anxiety often makes people put their proverbial foot in it because they blurt out revelations unthinkingly to cover up their nervousness.

Test the water with innocuous disclosure about yourself. This could be, for example, your birthplace rather than your birth date and your profession or trade rather than the rung of the career ladder you are on. Keep away from issues that may be emotionally laden for the other person, such as births, divorces, deaths and disease. Also be aware of any potential sensitive spots arising from their gender and cultural background.

251 Avoid jokes

Your self-esteem won't flourish under the icy stares and embarrassing silence that occurs when one falls flat. By all means collect funny true stories and witty quotations. These are much less risky, but be aware that they can also be quite self-revealing.

252 Search for similarities in people you find daunting

When you feel in awe of someone and find yourself getting tongue-tied with them, look for ways in which they are the same as you. These could be physical attributes, personality characteristics or skills. Or it could be something about their personal background such as their family life or a place where they have lived. If you can talk to them about a shared interest or experience, so much the better.

253   Hallucinate with humorous friends

When you feel yourself slipping into your 'too serious' mood or a panic state, hear voices. Imagine hearing the voices of friends with a great sense of humour. What might they be telling you to do or say in this situation? You can also trying 'listening' to the voices of your favourite comedians. You can be sure that they will take the sting out of the situation and help you to gain a sense of perspective.

254 Know the rules of your relationship

All good personal relationships have their own set of rules, though they are rarely written down. Break-downs and break-ups result when these rules are not respected. If you are unsure of the rules in your relationship, have the courage to discuss the subject before it is too late. You can use this list as a starting point. It is based on some basic principles that seem to guide happy marriages.

★ mutual trust;
★ respect for each other's privacy;
★ emotional support;
★ fidelity;
★ equitable sharing of household expenses and chores;
★ looking after each other in times of illness and misfortune;
★ showing interest in each other's activities;
★ allowing each other to have some independence;
★ keeping confidences;
★ personal feelings about each other;
★ talking about problems concerning the relationship;
★ never being violent;
★ agreeing before major expenditure of joint finances.

255   Nourish your partnership

Your marriage or partnership will only be as nourishing for you as you are to it! So ask yourself:

★ Do you compliment each other frequently?
★ Do you continue to specify why you love each other?
★ How many celebrations of successes have you had this year?
★ Do you ever give surprise presents?
★ Are your special days special enough?
★ Are you giving yourself enough time to be alone together?
★ How often do you use cuddles and hugs to express love rather than just to stimulate each other sexually?

Show your answers to your partner; talk and make some resolutions!

Does your partner repeatedly do something or act in a way that damages your self-esteem? If so, talk about it with your partner. Don't be afraid that it will kill your romance. In fact, not challenging put-downs is what does that. You may find your partner hasn't even realized they were hurting you. Put-downs are sometimes a cultural habit that people are not even aware of.

Above all, don't buy the argument that you are being 'too sensitive'. If a put-down hurts your self-esteem, then it should be stopped – and anybody worth loving will appreciate that fact.

257 Don't expect your partner to read your mind

There is no truth in the myth that because we love someone we automatically know what they need or want. So don't continue feeling hurt or unlovable if your partner isn't picking up your hints or anticipating your needs or preferences. Be clear about what you like and don't like. But when you get surprised with a present that isn't quite right, accept it gracefully and enjoy the love with which it was given.

258   Accept that great sex doesn't necessarily flow from great love

It takes confidence to get what you want in a sexual relationship. That is partly because you have to admit that you are not perfect! (You may need help and advice.) It is also partly because you may have to be 'pushy' in order to get your needs met. (You may need to give ultimatums and initiate confrontations if you cannot negotiate.)

If your sex life isn't fulfilling, before talking to your partner about it you could prepare yourself by:

★ Helping to beat any feelings of ignorance and embarrassment by buying or borrowing relevant books;
★ Reawakening your body to sensual pleasure by having a massage;
★ Masturbating if you are frustrated;
★ Talking to a friend about your difficulty;
★ Reading sexy literature;
★ Booking an appointment with a counsellor – many now have special training in sexual problems and would be happy to give an initial counselling session with just one partner.

259   Be prepared for a break-up

If you feel divorce or separation is in any way a possibility, don't just hope it will never happen; prepare for it – just in case. If it does happen and you are unprepared, your self-esteem will plummet even further and then you will be less able to stand up for your rights in the negotiation process.

Make sure you have good answers for these questions:

★ Who can I turn to for support? Have I enough friends who wouldn't feel torn between us? Would my family support me or would they disapprove?
★ How would I survive financially? Do I need my own resources to fall back on? What about my pension rights?
★ Where would I live? Is the house or flat in joint names? Is there somewhere I could go for temporary shelter if necessary?
★ If a crisis occurred, would we try to hide everything from the children or do we believe in keeping them informed? How would we ensure they were not used as weapons between us?
★ Do I know my legal rights and have I access to a good solicitor?

260 Don't feel obliged to repay every kindness

There are probably many people who have sensed your distress and difficulties. They may genuinely want to give you help without any expectation of a return for their kindness. Maybe they feel 'blessed' by their own good fortune or maybe their desire to help is purely altruistic.

Try to take their kindness with good grace. Enjoy and treasure this privilege – and the compliment that goes with it. (People rarely choose to help those they consider to be undeserving or unworthy of help.)

You may not be in a position to repay the kindness you are shown, but if you are, think twice about it. The person who gave to you from the heart might be even more impressed if you gave to someone else in need when you are able to do so.

261   Don't party if you are not a party animal

Parties and social gatherings are hell for many people – and they can seriously damage self-esteem. If you don't have an extrovert personality or are not wearing the latest fashion accessory, you may find yourself quite unfairly ostracized. Don't put yourself through this kind of experience until your self-esteem can handle it.

It is often much easier to strike up new friendships while you are doing something with other people. This is especially so if you are doing an activity which you both love. It is common knowledge that adult education classes, sports clubs, political parties, pressure groups and business networks have friendship-making as an important 'hidden agenda'. The internet or your local library will have a catalogue of all the clubs and societies in your area. Almost all will agree to people coming along to one meeting before joining, so you can do the rounds before making a commitment.

262   Keep well away from dating agencies until you are strong

You need strong self-esteem and bags of social confidence to make the best of these. The experience of throwing yourself into this kind of competitive game could make you feel even worse about yourself. Although most will unscrupulously welcome you with open arms and seductive offers, be wary. There are much better ways to spend your money and less torturous ways to meet people. You can always join an agency later when your confidence is stronger. They can be an excellent means to meet people who you would never have a chance of meeting otherwise.

263   Start each working day with an enjoyable activity

Try to arrive at work 10 minutes early so that you can do something you enjoy first. For example, a leisurely read of the paper or a cup of coffee with a colleague. This will help to set your mind in a positive mood.

As stressful as work can be, it should always be possible to achieve this aim. A laugh will help you relax and maintain a positive outlook. You will also work faster and think more creatively. Laughter also acts as social glue so you will have much better relationships with colleagues. And if you are the person that makes sure this happens, you will be very popular.

If you work in isolation on your own, allow yourself some light relief with an amusing book, radio or TV programme.

265 Ensure your work is meeting your psychological needs

Of course, no one can expect work to be totally satisfying 100% of the time. For the sake of your self-esteem, however, it should be satisfying a fair proportion of your psychological needs – as well as your need for money. Check that it is doing this for you and, if it isn't, consider some changes to ensure that it does.

Note down 10 psychological needs that you would like to be satisfied through your work. For instance, these could be:

learning
stimulation
innovation
independence
autonomy
recognition
achievement
responsibility
security
creation.

Reflect on how well your current job is meeting these needs. Think about what you might need to do in order to get more of these needs met in your current work. Are any fears stopping you from making these changes? If so, write them down and note an action you could take to help you control this fear. (For example, if you have a fear of failure, remind yourself what you have learnt from past mistakes.)

266 Be flexi-minded about your working life

Working nine to five in the one job, five days a week, isn't for everyone. If your full-time job isn't working out, consider the variety of other working arrangements available, such as flexi-time, annual hours (to be done whenever and wherever), job-sharing, contract, freelance or you could try finding two part-time jobs. Know what working style suits you and try to find it for yourself. Only then will you be able to fulfil your true potential.

267 Check your contribution is making a difference

For a job to be satisfying, at the very least we must feel that what we are doing is worthwhile. Even if we are the tiniest cog in a gigantic global production wheel, we must know that our contribution counts and believe that the end result of our effort will make a difference to someone or something. If we don't think that we are doing a meaningful job, our mental health (and therefore our quality of life) suffers. The moment we stop feeling useful, our self-esteem takes a nosedive. That's why redundancy and retirement can spark off depression and self-destructive habits.

Sometimes jobs and roles become out-of-date without the organization realizing that this has happened. If you do not feel that the job you do is as necessary or important as it used to be, don't just continue because you think you are getting paid for 'an easy ride'. Talk to someone about your concerns. This could be to your boss, the human resources department or your union or professional body. But, before speaking, think of ways in which your role could be changed to make it more effective, otherwise you could talk your way out of a job.

This might be taking a 10-minute break to go for a short walk, finding a private place to do some stretching exercises or simply tuning out for 5 minutes. You may not think you have the time or the need to do to do this, but you will be much more productive if you do. You will also be able to cope with much more pressure. (But that is a secret you may want to keep from your boss!)

269 Say 'Yes' to new opportunities

However fearful, unusual or odd-sounding a new challenge sounds, give it a go. You have probably been playing too safe with your talents while your self-esteem has been low. Make it clear to those concerned that this is your first time, ask for help and support, and any cover you need. Then go for it. You can only learn from failure and grow in confidence as a result of an unexpected success. People will admire you for having the courage to 'have a go' – and so they should!

270 Be specific when criticizing others – or the organization

One golden rule when giving criticism is to avoid generalizations. For example, it is more useful to say, 'You've overspent on your budget three times this year', rather than, 'You're a poor manager.'

271 Acknowledge the positive before tackling the negative

Even if you have a problem with a system or a machine, this tip will help. For example, if your computer has frozen yet again, the temptation is to swear at it and wish no one had ever invented the things. You may start to think of all the other times it has let you down and how much easier life was before you had one. However true this may or may not be, this negative attitude is not going to help you to solve your current problem. Instead, just appreciating some of the good things that you would lose if you did not have a computer will help to click you back into a more reasonable and calm state.

This is even more important when dealing with people who are being difficult. People are less easy to replace and have feelings and reputations that can be damaged if we approach the problem in an unnecessarily negative frame of mind. So, before confronting them, start with an appreciation of some aspect of their character or work.

272 Be happy to work with people who are different to you

Unlike in our social life, we are stuck with the people we work with. Many of these might be people who are very different from you in personality and values. This could be good for you both personally and professionally. A working team of different kinds of people is usually the strongest and most effective kind of team. This is not just because the individuals have different skills and attitudes to offer, but because they extend the potential of each other. Working with someone who is arrogant and extrovert could force you to become more assertive and socially skilled.

273　Empathize if you want to be heard

Everyone automatically pricks up their ears and opens their hearts when someone tunes into their feelings or problems. So before making a request or saying something the other person may not want to hear, empathize. Say something that indicates that you are aware of their feelings and/or problems. For example, 'I appreciate that you have a limited budget, but I need ...' or 'I realize what I'm going to say might be disappointing for you, but I do prefer ...')

This applies to both negative and positive feedback. (We need to look confident when giving compliments, otherwise they embarrass both the receiver and the giver.)

Take at least three deep breaths, but if you have time, do some stretches and a mini-meditation to relax you even more.

275 Use your own carrots to motivate you

Take responsibility for keeping yourself inwardly motivated. Use encouraging self-talk and promises of treats to be arranged by you and you alone. The less dependent you are on inducements from others, the more confident you will feel. You can still ask for your 'just rewards' from others when you deserve them, but you will be more likely to get them if you are already feeling amply self-rewarded.

276 Keep a watchful eye on your body when criticizing someone

You may be putting forward a very well-rehearsed and reasonable speech, but if you are nervous or angry your body might be giving off aggressive signals. If it is, the other person will respond defensively and will not really be listening to what you are saying. You should check that your legs and arms are loose and not crossed, that you are sitting upright and not forward and that you are not staring or glaring. Your voice should not be rising and should be evenly paced. If you notice your voice is beginning to squeak, pause and take a couple of deep breaths.

277 Place your fingertips together for composure

This is a quick way of filling yourself with a sense of confidence and calm.

Make a V shape with your hands. Place your fingertips so that each is touching the corresponding tip of the other hand. Slightly stretch your fingers and let your hands hang loosely in front of you pointing downwards if you are standing. If you are sitting place them in the same position on your knees.

Take a few slow deep breaths and feel how centred and composed you are.

This is a body position that many confident people naturally take up when they are relaxed or when they want to compose themselves before speaking to an audience. It is also used in some yoga positions.

You will make much more of an impression if you do not wander around a subject. This is very easy to do when you are nervous. Check that you are not including unnecessary waffle, examples and justifications. The simpler your speech, the easier it is to listen to.

279 Avoid using the label 'difficult people'

This is not helpful for you or the other person. Also, it is stigmatizing and unfair. People are rarely difficult all of the time to all people. Indeed, they may only be difficult in their relationship with you. Other people may not find them at all difficult.

Refer instead to the specific behaviour that you find difficult. For example, their untidiness, irresponsible use of money or their short-fuse responses.

Lend your support to a campaign for an improvement in your organization. You don't have to have charisma, or shout loudly or be a wonderful orator to be a campaigner for the common good. Leaders are usually much more grateful for help in the background. Offer your support without putting yourself down, by outlining first what you cannot do. Say what you are good at and leave it up to them to find a role for you. That way you will know that you are giving in the very best way and your efforts will be most appreciated.

You may think this is impossible to do, but most people have enough control over their working schedule to be able to do this. If you can arrange, for example, to do some simple administrative tasks or work on a project you enjoy at the end of the day, you will leave in a calmer and more relaxed frame of mind. If you leave in a negative stressed-out state, you will not enjoy your evening or weekend as much, and will not return to work in a positive frame of mind.

If you need to persuade your boss this is a good idea, explain that you believe you will not give of your best to difficult tasks at the end of the day. Say that generally you would prefer to make sure you deal with certain matters when you are refreshed and working on maximum energy. Obviously, you must also indicate that you will be prepared to make an exception to this rule when a real crisis occurs.

Spirituality is the new 'intelligence' that leading edge companies are now seeking to engender in their workplaces. They know that a spiritually dead environment is not conducive to bringing out the best in people. They also know that, increasingly, people are not prepared to sell their souls for the sake of business. This is good news for people like you who know the danger of disrespecting your personal values and ideals.

Some employers are now providing meditation and prayer rooms. Others are putting up spiritually uplifting posters or inviting gurus to give uplifting talks about values and high ideals.

Whatever meaning the word 'spirit' has for you, make sure that it has a place in your work as well. Keep a reminder on your desk or wall if you need to do so. This could be a photo of a stunning landscape, a quote or a prayer, or a symbolic stone or crystal that will help you to keep a spiritual perspective.

283   Make your journey home as calm as it can be

Of course, we often want to leave work in a rush and get home by the quickest route possible. But maybe this habit is not doing much good for your health and self-esteem. If your journey involves being pushed and shoved in a crowded train, or being constantly cut-up on a motorway by aggressive drivers, it certainly isn't.

Think about alternative (though slightly longer) options, or wait until the rush hour has finished – at least sometimes. If you do not have much control over your route, ensure that you have a good book or magazine to read, or calming music to play to yourself. Alternatively, use your waiting and travelling time to do some simple meditation or to reflect on what you have done well that day. Whatever happens, don't use that time for worrying needlessly about matters that you cannot resolve until your next working day.

284 Remember your body speaks louder than your voice

If you cannot find the words, you can always send a message with your body. You can *look* interested, concerned, impressed and willing, even if you cannot get a word in edgeways. Equally, you can send the wrong message by looking deadpan and straight-faced even without opening your mouth and putting your foot in it.

Adrenaline is supposed to be generated when we need short bursts of extra energy. It is dangerous to keep it pumping around your body for long periods. While we are in the 'high' state it engenders, our bodies are not doing their normal repair and maintenance work. This means that you will tire much more quickly, even though your adrenalin buzz makes you feel as though you have unlimited energy. This is when we can make some serious mistakes. Many work problems do not deserve a quick emergency response from us; they need to be tackled in a thoughtful, calm, step-by-step way. At work, if you feel you are firefighting all the time, you are not giving of your best and so your self-esteem will suffer.

Check if your pulse and heart rate are racing when they don't need to be doing so. If they are, use a relaxation technique to calm you down and reduce your adrenaline levels.

When we are under pressure, we often extend our potential. That is one of the reasons that employers push people. As someone with low self-esteem, it is likely that you will not think you have much potential to extend, so it is hard to think positively. It may help to think back to a time in the past when being under pressure produced a positive result. There must have been some time in your life when you achieved more than you thought you were capable of because you were pushed. Bring the memory of that occasion alive in your imagination. Visualize the colours and shapes; recall the scents, sounds and textures. Then consciously intensify the image as though you were seeing it on a giant cinema screen with digital sound. Your brain will automatically switch over from its negative mode into a more positive one and you will cope better as a result.

287   Get inspired before cracking the hardest nuts

Before starting on a particularly difficult project, dip into an autobiography or watch a video about a successful person. Better still, talk to someone who has achieved something you admire in real life. Don't ask for their advice, merely listen to their story. It will inspire you to do your very best.

288 Insist on quality time for difficult decisions

Making a difficult decision requires time, but not just any time, it must be good thinking time. When we are stressed or depressed our brain's capacity to think constructively is seriously impaired. Hard choices need a *quality* decision from you, so don't grab 5 minutes here and there to make them. You do not need any more regrets in your life.

Set aside at least 20 minutes solely for the purpose of making your decision. This will give you the time to wind your body down, before weighing up the pros and cons. Take yourself, whenever possible, into a peaceful environment where you won't be distracted or interrupted.

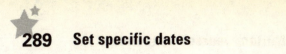

289 Set specific dates

When planning tasks and projects, always use specific dates rather than 'sooner' or 'later' and constantly review these. This will ensure that you keep to your targets and give of your best.

Many modern work environments are quite clinical and sterile in the their appearance. This may be a very appropriate 'look' and good for business, but often it is not very nurturing for the soul (especially one that may feel a little lost at times!). A reminder of nature or a brief face-to-face contact with it may help you to restore perspective and calm your nerves. Nature deserves its reputation as a great healer and its fees are eminently affordable. You could have a calendar or pictures of uplifting scenery, or maybe a small plant on your desk. Alternatively, you could ensure that you take a walk around a local park or garden, or listen to a CD of natural sounds at least once or twice a week.

291   Keep reminding yourself of your strengths

When our self-esteem is low, we lose sight of our strengths, so sometimes we have to give ourselves a reminder. Do this exercise and keep its results in a place where you glance at them from time to time.

Think of five successes you have had in your working life to date. Take a piece of paper and divide it into six columns. Head one column 'strengths' and each of the others with one of the successes you have chosen. (You can include some skills that you regard as strengths in this column as well.) Now select the following:

★ Three key mental strengths that helped you achieve each success (for example: creativity, planning and common sense).
★ Three physical strengths or characteristics that helped you (for example: speed, coordination and strength).
★ Three interpersonal skills that helped you achieve each success (for example: listening, leadership and compassion).
★ Three key character traits or personal qualities that have helped you (for example: persistence, honesty and courage).
★ Three broad categories of knowledge or wisdom (for example, mathematical knowledge, life experience and knowledge of literature).
★ Three learned skills (for example: your ability to ride horses, car maintenance and specific academic or professional training).

292 Aim to use the strengths that you enjoy most

Which of your strengths do you enjoy using most? Ask yourself if your current work gives you enough opportunity to make the most of these. Try to ensure that it does, because if you use these strengths you are more likely to thrive.

293   Be your own 'Head of Training'

You must take care that you are receiving the training you
need, not just for the company's own current good, but for
your career as well. Don't go on courses that you think will
waste your time. It is a pointless exercise to go on a course
that you think you don't really need. Argue your case for
going on ones that will truly extend your potential or give
you the skills you need to do your job better. You may have
to do your own research to find out what is available. Don't
forget that some training departments are not familiar with
what is needed at the 'coalface'. They are often 'sold'
unsuitable courses, maybe for the wrong reasons such as
being the latest 'fad' or because they are cheap.

In the current economic climate, your employer is unlikely to give you as much training as you need. Cutbacks always hit this side of an organization's budget first. But you have to think ahead – especially if your employer is hitting hard times! Make sure that you are getting training for the skills that could be of use to you in the next and subsequent stages of your career. To do this you may need to set aside some of your own money to give yourself extra training. You may need more help than colleagues who are more confident. A few one-to-one sessions with a trainer or a weekend course from time to time could bolster your self-esteem and help you to learn better on the courses which your organization provides. Alternatively, keep up-to-date with self-help books, internet courses or cassettes in your car.

When our self-esteem is low, people perceive us as being vulnerable. This may inhibit them from giving you the feedback you need. In this case you may have to ask for some. But make sure you do it in a way that means they won't over-protect you. Tell them straight that you need honest feedback, even if it hurts at first. Also, tell them to give you specific feedback that is helpful, rather than over-generalized comments or subjective opinion. For example, if someone says: 'I don't think you are using your full potential', ask them to clarify that comment. Ask them for examples and ideas. This may sound difficult to do, but it is essential and it will be a lot easier to do the second time around when you realize how much more helpful this kind of feedback is.

Be very honest in the way you write this. Try to see yourself through the objective eyes of someone who is valuing you merely in terms of the contribution you could make to the organization's future, the bottom line and the working team as a whole.

Note what you may need to do to ensure that the next time you do this exercise, the reference you write will be truly a glowing one.

297 Relax before going into a meeting

This is especially important if you are nervous about making a presentation or talking in a meeting. Doing this one-minute relaxation will make all the difference to your performance and confidence.

Focus your attention on your breathing, which should be deep and leisurely from your stomach. Slowly repeat a simple calming mantra to yourself several times, in time with your breathing. (For example, on your in-breath say 'I am ...' and on your out-breath, '... calm.' If you have time, in your mind's eye visualize a calming scene such as the corner of a quiet garden, swans gliding on a lake or the sleeping face of a loved one. Recall the sounds and scents as well (for example, the smell of newly mown grass, the ripple of water or the whisper of gentle breathing).

Maybe your low self-esteem is warping your view of your real potential or holding you back from exploring every possible avenue. Make regular searches on the internet to see what is happening in the area that interests you. Find a way to go to relevant conferences where you could meet inspiring as well as directly useful contacts. Make sure that your training is relevant to your dream job as well as your current one.

Keep your dream job alive in your mind and others' minds by sharing it as much as you can. You just never know who may know of an opportunity that could be useful to you.

299 Ensure your environment is helping you to give your best

Over the next week, observe yourself in action within your work environment. Notice any frustrations, distractions or depressing features such as noise, uncomfortable chairs, clutter, lack of natural light or views of the outside world, or if the air-conditioning or heating is too high or low. Make a list of what you need to do to improve your environment. (For example, put aside a morning for a clearout and ask for the heating to be turned down.)

When you find yourself feeling negatively inclined towards an opportunity or a problem, use this strategy. I have called it GEE to help you remember the three common irrational thinking habits which may be affecting your outlook – Generalizing, Exaggerating and Excluding.

Ask yourself the following questions. If your answer to any of them is 'yes', then restate your thoughts in a more positive way.

1   Am I generalizing from a specific experience? For example:
    Irrational: 'Last time I tried this it was a disaster. Don't give it to me to do – I'm bound to mess it up.'
    Rational: 'I didn't do this very well last time, but the chances are I will have learned from my mistake and will do a better job this time.'

2   Am I exaggerating current problems or potential hazards or difficulties? For example:
    Irrational: 'This is an impossible task.'
    Rational: 'This is a challenging task.'

3   Am I excluding any positive aspects or potential? For example:
    Irrational: 'There's no point in me applying for that job. They'll think I'm too old.'
    Rational: 'My chances are not great for this particular job, but they may be the kind of organization that needs people with experience. I have nothing to lose from trying.'

301 Use quotes to top up your optimism

Regularly dip into a book of motivational quotes that you keep handy on your desk or in your briefcase. Record your favourites onto a cassette and listen to them on your journey to work.

302   **Broadcast your deadlines for decisions**

When our self-esteem is low, we often lose confidence in our ability to make good decisions. Next time you are finding it difficult to make a decision at work, try giving yourself a deadline and letting your colleagues know the date.

303 Maintain an upright posture

This is good for your back, your inner esteem and your outer confidence. Every so often, check your posture by imagining that someone is pulling a string in the top of your head directly upwards.

304   Beware of work snacks and 'treats'

Many workplaces are places full of tempting sugary snacks that we know are not good for us. When we are stressed and see others eating them, it is hard to resist them. You know that each time you give in you are damaging your self-esteem. Avoid the temptation by having some healthy alternatives, such as bags of nuts and dried fruit, always ready at hand.

305 Do early morning relaxations on difficult days

When you know you have a hard day ahead, set your alarm clock 15 minutes early and do this relaxation before going to work.

For a few minutes do some slow stretches to release some of the tension from your muscles. Then lie or sit in a well-supported position and loosen all your limbs. Close your eyes and visualize your breath passing into your body and through your lungs. Create a picture in your mind of your heart throbbing as it pumps oxygenated blood into your arteries. Watch this pumping action gradually become slower and slower as you breathe more deeply and evenly. Notice how your pulse has quietened. Now tighten and very slowly release each of the following sets of muscles one by one: toes, calves, thighs, bottom, stomach, chest, shoulders, fingers, arms, neck, jaw, eyes and, finally, forehead.

Notice the sense of lightness in your body. Focus your attention back on your breathing for a few moments. Now imagine you are on your own lying on a Lilo in a quiet, beautiful, sheltered pool. Feel the warmth of the sun on your skin as you gently float around in the water.

As you lie there in the pool, imagine yourself successfully doing whatever it is you want to do during the day. Continue watching yourself for a few more minutes and feel the sense of contentment and pleasure your achievement brings. Slowly deepen your breathing and bring your attention back to the real world. Open your eyes and stay still for a few minutes before getting up.

306   Carry a stress ball in your coat pocket

Whenever you have a boring moment in a queue or on transport, you can squeeze and release your stress ball. This will help you to release your tension.

307 Prioritize, prioritize and prioritize

Set your priorities every morning before you start work and ensure that you stick to them routinely each day. Breaking away from your priorities should be a rare exception. If it isn't, then you know you are not in the driving seat of your own life. Maybe you need to be more assertive, or even look for a new job.

308 Network even when you don't appear to need to

Right now you may not be looking for another job, extra clients or more staff, but you never know when that day might come. Take every opportunity to meet new people and find out more about them and their interests and skills. Make sure that you go somewhere where you will meet new people at least once a month. This could be a conference, a network club or a talk.

309 Use secret stretches to stay relaxed

You can use the following technique at your desk or around a conference table when you need to relax your body discreetly.

Unwind your body by uncrossing your legs, dropping your shoulders and sitting up straight so that your body is more supported. Clench one or both of your fists secretly under the table and then slowly relax them. Repeat the same process with your feet and toes. No one will notice, but you will immediately feel more relaxed and in control, and you can be sure that when you speak your voice will project with more volume and impact because you are relaxed.

Maybe the super-confident can get away with doing this, but you shouldn't take the risk. These kind of comments are unnecessary and do not help to build up the impression of someone who can be relied upon. Try to avoid saying things like:

★ 'I'm surprised I got it finished on time. I was still struggling with it last night.'
★ 'I hope these figures are correct now. The first three times I did them, I came up with different answers.'
★ 'Oh, I nearly forgot to tell you – John rang today.'

311   Keep your pleas for prayer time

Emotional pleas are not for the workplace. Make sure you use objective facts and sound arguments to back up any request you make. Keep your tone of voice steady and strong and your body language confident, however nervous or frustrated you may feel.

Develop the habit of using waiting time productively. For example, revive the vision of your long-term ambition with some purposeful daydreaming; check your 'to do' list; reflect on your progress; rehearse in your head a difficult phone call you need to make; or just calmly repeat self-esteem building affirmations.

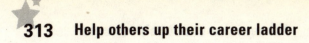

313 Help others up their career ladder

Do this just because it will give you a buzz of satisfaction. The add-on benefits will come for free. Your self-esteem will get an instant boost and you will be storing up favours that may come in handy at a later date. Show your colleagues any training or job opportunities that you have spotted and they may have missed. Introduce them to people whom you think they need to know.

Not every company will allow you to do this, but try to persuade yours of the advantages of doing so. It may be possible to add an extra printed line under your name that specifies your particular interests or specialisms. If this is not possible, do this by hand before handing over your card. Alternatively, jot down a word or two on the back which will remind them of what you were discussing or need to know.

Wherever you are going, leave plenty of time for the unexpected to occur en route. Confident people may get away with a just-in-time approach, but you will simply feel and look, flustered and inept when you arrive late. If you get there early, you can use the time to do some positive affirmations, relaxation or revision.

317 Update your CV regularly

This is a great confidence-building exercise and so much easier to do nowadays as most people have theirs on a computer. Add in your recent achievements and training events. Every so often, re-vamp its appearance as well. The style of CVs changes, and you need to keep yours looking up-to-date.

318 Compliment your colleagues without expectation of return

Giving compliments is good for your self-esteem, so don't waste any opportunities just because someone else is too mean or too stressed to be kind to you.

319 When wearing an 'eye-catcher', be prepared to talk

If you don't want to say anything or be approached by strangers at a meeting or conference, look bland. But if you want to make an impression, choose to wear or carry something which could provoke a comment. This could be an unusual tie, brooch or article of clothing. Alternatively, you could carry a certain newspaper or book. Be ready to answer questions in a confident and interesting way about your eye-catching item. This is a very good networking trick and will help you be remembered. It is also a good way of handling tricky first conversations and keeps you in control of that invaluable first impression.

Be fun to be with, but not always at your own expense. Of course, it is good to laugh at yourself sometimes, but when our self-esteem is low, we can do it too often and then get stuck in the role. Clowns give pleasure to others, but often end up feeling very sad and depressed inside. We may love them when we need them, but they become irritating and dispensable when we are not in the mood or serious business needs to be done.

321 Be a copycat

When you see someone behaving or speaking in a way that you admire, don't become caught up in your envy. Instead, start noting the specific words and body language your 'role model' is using. When you get home, practise copying the way they were acting and repeat what they said in the tone of voice they used. You are not training yourself to be a carbon copy of them in real life – you must, of course, be you and develop your own individual style. But the exercise will help to build up your confidence. It works because it reminds us that confident behaviour is learned behaviour and not a gift that is magically given to a chosen few at birth.

322 Spread your toes and feel your heels

This is a tip from a Pilates instructor. It almost sounds too simple to be true, but don't dismiss it until you have tried it because it has worked wonders for me. It will help release the tension in your back, regain a sense of balance and feel more confident and in control.

Stand tall with your feet in line with your hips. Spread your toes and feel the ground beneath you with each – particularly your big toe. Then feel your heels on the floor. Gently rock back and forth from your toes to your heels until you find your ideal central position.

323 Let time-wasters waste themselves

Be firm when people are wasting your time. Don't chat any longer than you want simply out of fear of being 'rude' or 'unkind'. Watch and be inspired by confident people. They protect their time by stating clearly and politely that they wish to resume their work or that the matter in question is not their responsibility. They rarely add an apology for doing so.

324 Say 'Sorry' once and once only

People with low self-esteem almost always over-apologize. This does not endear you to others and does nothing towards rectifying your mistake. In a working environment particularly, all anyone should be interested in is that you have acknowledged your mistake and learned from it or taken steps to rectify any damage done.

325 Share your successes cautiously

Make a habit of sharing your successes with people who will be genuinely pleased for you and not secretly envious. For example, tell your boss rather than a low-achieving, competitive colleague about a difficult deal you managed to clinch.

326 Insist on quality time for quality projects

Refuse to rush work you know is ultra-important. To do anything else is self-defeating and bad for business of any description. If you want your refusal to be respected, you must also be prepared to do work in a 'good-enough' way on tasks that are less important when asked to do so.

327 Keep an eye-mask and earplugs in your desk or briefcase

These will enable you to find some peace whenever you need it wherever you are. Use them regularly, especially when you are in stressful noisy environments.

328 Choose companies that share your values

Obviously, this is not always possible but try to keep it as general rule. The closer your values are to the companies' that you deal with or employ you, the more self-respect, motivation and success you will have.

329 Beware of taking decisions too personally

Remember, in the world of work most decisions are business or organizational decisions. For better or worse, the people making them are rarely thinking about their impact on the feelings or welfare of individual 'cogs' in the wheel. When our self-esteem is low, we tend to take things much too personally, so you may find yourself feeling guilty or personally slighted when you have no need to do so.

330 Don't push yourself beyond your attention span

Remember that your attention span is usually shorter than you'd like to think. Research indicates that it is likely to be around 20 minutes, but it often varies with the time of day. Once you have passed your 'threshold', remember you are more likely to start making mistakes and stop registering data in your memory.

331 Carry a mascot

If Luciano Pavarotti still needs to carry his white hankie on stage, why shouldn't you have a lucky charm or two to steady you? A highly successful friend of mine always puts on a tie with an elephant design when he is particularly nervous before a presentation. Sometimes he even tells his audience he has done so, as he believes that this helps to calm his nerves even more.

332 Count the cost to your self-esteem before giving in

Bowing to unfair pressure erodes your self-esteem. Remind yourself of the damage low self-esteem is already doing to your life and what you stand to lose if you don't protect its reserves. Then ask yourself if you can afford to give in. The long-term costs must outweigh the immediate short-term gain.

333 Share your non-work achievements

Don't wait to include these on your next CV. These may well stand you in good stead with your current colleagues and bosses. They may even impress them more than your achievements in work to date. Your impressive golf handicap or prize for juggling may make you stand out in a way that you have not been able to do before. They may also indicate that you have potential that has not yet been fully tapped in the course of your work.

334   Use reminder cards unashamedly

Before going into a meeting or interview, put all your key points onto reminder cards. Glance at these from time to time and just before you leave to ensure that you have said everything you wanted to say. Do not apologize for looking at your cards or look at them in a furtive way. Say in a confident manner that you would just like to check your notes to make sure that everything has been covered.

336 **Deal with the subversive enemies of concentration**

Instead of berating yourself for poor concentration, check that there isn't an underlying reason for it wandering more than it should. Remind yourself of the following:

★ Your body must be free of tension, but in an energized rather than deeply relaxed state. It must also be fed with the best fuel, including fresh, organic foods that have not been processed.
★ Your mind must be lively, but also well under your control. Use meditation and positive self-talk to stop it racing, flitting, getting stuck or going blank.
★ Your environment should be appropriately conducive to concentration. Check that its ambience, atmosphere and noise levels are as helpful as they can be.

337 Resist becoming the office martyr

You will not do yourself any favours in the long term by being too willing to do what nobody else wants to do. In spite of smiling appearances, martyrs do not earn respect. They collect secret disrespect. Sooner or later a crisis will make this lack of appreciation very apparent.

Bullying at work is on the increase. Don't feel ashamed if you are being bullied and don't consider it to be just your personal problem. Bullies at work rarely have only one victim. If you speak up about your problem to colleagues, you will almost certainly find that others have suffered. The fact that they have chosen to stay silent doesn't mean that you have to do so too.

If you have done your 'assertive best' to stand up for yourself, don't hesitate to call in extra help. Most victims need this. Find someone who will act as an effective and confident champion to your case. This could be either a senior colleague, someone from the Human Resource department, or your union or professional association. Alternatively, use the internet to find a self-help or campaigning organization.

339 Be prepared to step outside your job description

If you spot a problem that you think you can fix in someone else's department, don't be afraid to offer help. If someone is too proud to listen to advice from outside, perhaps they should not be in that job. It goes without saying that your advice must be offered in a respectful way. If it is, trust that the vast majority of people would be more than grateful to receive it.

340 Stand up when making or taking difficult phone calls

Put both feet firmly on the ground and pull yourself up tall. If you can, walk around as well. This will help to keep you relaxed, confident and sounding energetic. It will also give your voice more resonance and impact.

341 Don't make excuses for wanting to get a life

You deserve to have a balanced life for yourself. Don't use excuses about needy children, demanding partners or ailing mothers to get the free time you are entitled to. Also, don't be tempted to invent sicknesses. These can backfire on you and do nothing to build your esteem.

342 Make sure your chosen image has repetitive impact

Select three adjectives that sum up the main message you want to present about yourself and your work or products. (such as, 'organized', 'creative' and 'confident'). Ask yourself if you are currently conveying the three elements in this message in every way in which you make an impact. This includes your body language, your dress, the style of your office and the presentation of your work.

343   Keep a work notebook at home

Remember, our best ideas for solutions often come when we are relaxing rather than working, so keep a work notebook handy by your bed and sofa. Once you have jotted down your idea, try to forget about it until your next working day!

344   Think positively about conflict

Conflict can stimulate new ideas and help maintain high energy levels if it is managed well. All good managers know this and often try to stimulate conflict amongst their team. This is very hard on people with low self-esteem who tend immediately to take fright because they feel they haven't the confidence to fight their corner. Try to stay calm and positive when you feel a conflict is about to erupt. Do not try to avoid it or rush in too quickly to make your peace. Instead, tell yourself that conflicts can be highly constructive and a sign that people care.

345 Never think you are too old to change

'It is never too late to be what you might have been.'

GEORGE ELIOT

From time to time, you may need to check that you are projecting your voice as well as you can. Low self-esteem automatically sets our tone too high and often gives our voice an unpleasant squeak. A few deep-breathing exercises that push down your diaphragm and expand your chest will get your voice back on the right track. If you can afford the luxury, take yourself to a singing or drama coach who will help you learn even more useful tricks to keep your voice consistently deep enough in its tone.

347 Have a fun lunch-break once a week

Ideally, make this half way through your working week. Go somewhere for lunch with someone who makes you smile.

348 Expect less support at times of high pressure

Even your kindest colleagues may not appreciate your efforts when they are stressed; the less kind may be downright disruptive. This is a side of human nature that hurts when we are feeling vulnerable. When we are confident we can laugh it off or give back 'as good as we get', but it will inevitably knock more holes into shaky self-esteem. Make sure during these times that you nurture yourself particularly carefully or find external sources of support.

350 **Welcome frustration with yourself**

See frustration with yourself as a sign that you know you could be doing better. But don't allow it to escalate into anger. Before it reaches this pitch, take time out to release your tension through exercise or meditation. Then try a new approach or seek advice.

351 Clear your surrounding clutter

Make your workplace look organized. Even if you know your way around the muddle on your desk or in your workroom, does looking at it fill you with pride? If it doesn't, vow to get it cleared and looking organized for your inner sake as well as your outer image.

There may be many injustices at your workplace that you do not have the power to put right. But you will feel a good deal better about yourself if, at the very least, you have spoken your mind. Avoid using sermonizing language, and instead use assertive and non-threatening comments such as:

★ 'I appreciate that the company must recruit the best people currently available for the job, but I would prefer to see more women on the board.'
★ 'I know that in this economic climate it is difficult to achieve, but I believe that our administrative staff deserve to have a 10% increase.'

353 Be 'cheeky' and seek out high-quality mentors

If there is not a mentoring scheme in your organization or if you are self-employed, find someone or several people who could act as mentors. Don't be afraid to approach busy successful senior colleagues. Most people will be flattered to be asked, even if they cannot give you the time and have to say 'no'. They may have ideas about who else you could try. At the very least, they will be impressed by your keenness to learn and improve.

If you have certain areas of your life or background that you wish to keep private, make sure that you can respond in a credible and confident manner should someone purposefully or inadvertently question you. If you do not want to use a 'white lie' or covering story, practise at home using a response such as 'I would rather not discuss that aspect of my life right now.' until it sounds confident and natural.

355   Beat worrying about your future with contingency planning

Ask yourself what are some of the worst scenarios you could face during the next few months and outline some specific contingency plans. For example:

> 'If I'm made redundant on Monday I will …
>
> … ask for some leave to start job-hunting.'
> … ring the bank to check my overdraft facilities and investment options for redundancy pay.'
> … update my CV and send it to companies I would like to work for as well as recruitment agencies.'

In the course of making this kind of plan, it will become obvious that there are many things that can be done immediately and this will help divert your attention from your worries.

356   **Don't be a slave to the telephone**

Take control of the conversation before it gets going. Don't be afraid to interrupt immediately with a clear statement about how long you can talk. If you know they are ringing before you are ready to respond to what they want to discuss, say at the outset that you will ring them back. Don't ever feel that because someone has rung you, you need to respond immediately.

357 Stand up for your breaks

Regular breaks are essential not just for your health, but also for your efficiency. Don't allow them to be encroached on by pushy colleagues or overly demanding bosses. No one will thank you in the long run for making mistakes as a result of being overtired and under-inspired. The negative effects of workplace stress are well known. Anyone worth working for nowadays will respect you for standing up to them on this account.

358   Take your honours gracefully

'The greatest reward in terms of psychological satisfaction comes through recognition – being seen to have achieved and having that achievement publicly recognized.'

ALLEN CARMICHAEL

359 Don't give up even if you intend to move on

You may have already decided that you are in the wrong job and are actively looking for another. In the meantime, don't give up trying to improve your current position. Doing this could not only make your working life more rewarding, but also boost your self-esteem and improve your chances of getting a good reference.

360   Don't be too proud to delegate

Humility is a quality of confident people. They do not need to feel indispensable in order to feel good about themselves. You will do yourself and your self-esteem no favours by hanging on to tasks that others could do just as well or better.

361 Check your time management

Take yourself on a time-management course or read a self-help book on the subject. Just doing the exercises (even if you have done them all before) will help you to re-assess and remind you of your priorities.

362 Take a leaf out of Nelson Mandela's book

'Our deepest fear is not that we are inadequate. Our deepest fear is that we are powerful beyond measure. It is our light, not our darkness that frightens us … playing small doesn't serve the world. There's nothing enlightening about shrinking so that other people won't feel secure around you. We are all meant to shine, as children do … as we let our own light shine, we unconsciously give other people permission to do the same. As we are liberated from our own fear, our presence automatically liberates others.'

MARION WILLIAMSON – QUOTED BY NELSON MANDELA
AT HIS INAUGURAL ADDRESS, 1994

363 Stay ever-ready for job interviews

You never know when you may need to prepare for an interview for either a new job, a promotion or just to hold on to the role you currently have. Make sure that you can do the following:

★ Summarize concisely all your strengths, skills and potential;
★ Divulge your weaknesses in a positive way;
★ Answer the embarrassing or difficult questions that otherwise you would be afraid to be asked.

If you cannot do these, find some help. Go for a browse in a good bookshop – there are many excellent books designed to help you prepare for interviews.

365 Keep the *Self-Esteem Bible* and its good companions handy

Self-esteem rarely stays stable for long. Make sure that this book and any others that have helped you are readily available. Dip into them for inspirational reminders whenever you encounter a knock from life.

How to contact Gael Lindenfield

To find out more about Gael Lindenfield's consultancy service, courses, talks and other books, please visit her website:

www.gaellindenfield.com

Alternatively, please write to her c/o her publishers at the following address:

ThorsonsElement
HarperCollins*Publishers* Ltd
77–85 Fulham Palace Road
London W6 8JB

In addition, you might like to visit:

The Gael Lindenfield Confidence Clinic

This is a website hosted by Ecademy, a global business and social networking website (www.ecademy.com). At the Confidence Clinic, you can find free confidence-building tips and advice on handling problem situations. For members of Ecademy, she also has an on-line consultancy and information service. You can access the clinic directly using the following URL:

www.thegaellindenfieldconfidenceclinic.com